MARTIN
AND
BOBBY

A JOURNEY TOWARD JUSTICE

Claire Rudolf Murphy

CHICAGO
REVIEW
PRESS

Published by Chicago Review Press Incorporated
814 North Franklin Street
Chicago, Illinois 60610
ISBN 978-1-64160-010-1

Library of Congress Cataloging-in-Publication Data
Names: Murphy, Claire Rudolf, author.
Title: Martin and Bobby : a journey toward justice / Claire Rudolf Murphy.
Description: Chicago, Illinois : Chicago Review Press Incorporated, [2018] |
    Includes bibliographical references and index. | Audience: Ages 10 and up.
Identifiers: LCCN 2018008903 (print) | LCCN 2018028043 (ebook) | ISBN
    9781641600118 (adobe pdf) | ISBN 9781641600125 (kindle) | ISBN
    9781641600132 (epub) | ISBN 9781641600101 | ISBN 9781641600101 (cloth)
Subjects: LCSH: King, Martin Luther, Jr., 1929–1968—Juvenile literature. |
    Kennedy, Robert F., 1925–1968—Juvenile literature. | African American
    civil rights workers—United States—Biography—Juvenile literature. |
    Politicians—United States—Biography—Juvenile literature. | Civil rights
    movements—United States—20th century—Juvenile literature. | United
    States—History—20th century—Juvenile literature.
Classification: LCC E840.6 (ebook) | LCC E840.6 .M87 2018 (print) | DDC
    323.0973/0904—dc23
LC record available at https://lccn.loc.gov/2018008903

Interior design: Sarah Olson

Printed in the United States of America
5 4 3 2 1

———— ★ ————

In memory of dear friends Pat Kling, John McDermott,
and Steve McKee and my brother Jim

———— ★ ————

Let us move on in these powerful days, these days of challenge to make America what it ought to be. We have an opportunity to make America a better nation.
   –Martin Luther King Jr., Memphis, Tennessee, April 3, 1968

In this difficult day, in this difficult time for the United States, it's perhaps well to ask what kind of a nation we are . . . and what direction we want to move in.
   –Robert F. Kennedy, Indianapolis, Indiana, April 4, 1968

CONTENTS

PART III: 1968

"WHAT KIND OF A NATION WE ARE"

On April 4, 1968, Senator Robert Kennedy spoke at a campaign rally in a black neighborhood in Indianapolis. But instead of telling the crowd why they should vote for him for president, he had to announce that violence had struck again. "I have sad news for you, sad news for all of our fellow citizens, and people who love peace all over the world. . . . Martin Luther King was shot and killed tonight in Memphis, Tennessee."

Dr. King was the most prominent leader in the civil rights movement. Now he was gone. Riots erupted in cities across the country. But that night in Indianapolis a miracle happened. Bobby Kennedy didn't address the crowd like a politician, but rather as a person who also knew the pain of great loss. He gave comfort at one of the darkest moments in our country's history.

He didn't blame people for feeling angry. He told them that they had a choice about "what kind of a nation we are and what direction we want to move in."

In 1968 America was a country at war, on its city streets and in the rice paddies of Vietnam. Every day, tensions between white and black Americans triggered violence. Footage of police brutality, war protests on college campuses, and soldiers fighting in Vietnam filled television screens every evening. People on both sides of the political divide were afraid and angry. During those difficult days Martin and Bobby both offered hope and a belief that America's integrity and decency could be restored.

In 1995 a memorial sculpture of the two men was erected on the spot where Bobby had spoken 27 years earlier.

His speech that tragic night forever linked the two men—Robert Francis Kennedy (RFK) and Martin Luther King Jr. (MLK)—deepening a legacy they already shared. Though not friends, the two men had grown to respect each other through years of push and pull over civil rights. By 1968 they walked the same path, fighting for an end to poverty and the Vietnam War. Their compassion and spiritual faith that had connected with so many Americans also connected them to each other.

Though admired by many, Martin and Bobby were also misunderstood and even hated; their lives ended violently and far too soon.

But 50 years later, their words and legacy live on, providing inspiration during another troubled time in our history.

This is the story of their journey toward justice.

1

"I THINK WE CAN DO BETTER"

Wednesday, April 3, 1968, 9:00 AM (EST)
Hartsfield Airport, Atlanta, Georgia
The pilot's voice crackled over the loudspeaker. "Ladies and gentlemen, we've had a bomb threat that necessitated a hand search of every piece of luggage. But we are finally cleared for takeoff."

"It looks like they won't kill me this flight," Martin Luther King Jr. said to Ralph Abernathy, as the plane finally taxied down the runway. He knew the bomb threat was due to his presence.

"Nobody's going to kill you, Martin," Ralph replied, even though both men knew that it could happen. Martin was in danger every time he appeared in public. He had received thousands of death threats since he'd taken on leadership of the emerging civil rights movement in 1954. Martin had no choice but to live with the fear if he wanted to continue his work and speak around the country.

After Martin and Ralph teamed up during the Montgomery bus boycott 13 years earlier, they formed the Southern Christian Leadership Conference (SCLC) to organize protests to end segregation in the South. The civil rights protests, boycotts, and sit-ins finally resulted in the 1964 Civil Rights Act that ended legal segregation. But four years later there was still much more to be done.

Martin stared out the window during the short flight to Memphis. It was his third visit to the city in recent weeks and meant yet more time away from his wife, Coretta, and their four children. Thirteen hundred sanitation workers

Seven thousand students flocked to Sproul Plaza at the University of California, Berkeley, to hear Martin speak in May 1967.

had gone on strike in February. Two months later the mayor was still ignoring the workers' requests for a living wage and safer working conditions, and Martin's old friend Jim Lawson had begged him to come to Memphis and support their cause.

Many of Martin's SCLC associates didn't think they had the time and resources to support both the sanitation strike and the upcoming Poor People's Campaign. Martin convinced them that the Memphis workers represented the very issues at stake in the new protest.

Martin knew that many civil rights activists were frustrated by a lack of progress and wanted to use more aggressive tactics. The slogans "Black Power!" and "Burn, baby, burn!" had taken hold, especially in communities of color.

Last week in Memphis 20,000 people had marched in support of the sanitation workers. But roving black teenagers who had not been trained in nonviolent protest disrupted the march, breaking windows at local stores and throwing rocks at the police. Officers responded with batons and tear gas, and later in the day they shot and killed teen Larry Payne, whom they suspected of looting.

Afterwards many in the press blamed Martin and questioned how he could lead a national campaign when a protest in Memphis had spiraled out of control. Martin had been depressed ever since, physically and emotionally exhausted. He wondered if nonviolence was dead.

Martin took time to pray and reflect. Then he renewed his commitment to nonviolent protest, just as he had so many other times over the years. This coming Monday he was determined to lead another demonstration, a peaceful one, to prove it could still be done.

In all these years Martin had seldom wavered in his belief that nonviolent protest was the most effective way to create change. Not by fighting or lashing out, but by silently, calmly resisting unjust laws and conditions. He believed he could prove that again when thousands of working poor people marched to Washington, DC, to lobby President Lyndon Baines Johnson (LBJ) and federal agencies to fund programs for housing, training, and new jobs. New York senator Robert Kennedy supported the Poor People's Campaign, and Martin was hopeful others in Congress would too.

Martin had long believed that poverty and a lack of opportunities were causing the uprisings in poor black neighborhoods. He knew the SCLC had to work with all races to find solutions. It had to turn poor people's power into a political movement. Thus the Poor People's Campaign was born.

But 1968 was a presidential election year, and reporters wanted to talk about that contest, not the new antipoverty protest. Every day they pestered Martin with questions. Which Democratic candidate would best serve civil rights concerns? What if the Republican Richard Nixon won the election? All the candidates wanted Martin's endorsement because of his influence with black voters. Martin had made no public statement. But privately he said that Senator Kennedy "would make a great president" and would be the best Democratic nominee because he was strong with working-class voters and minorities.

Martin should know. He had watched Bobby Kennedy change since his early days as attorney general under his brother, President John F. Kennedy. As Bobby's understanding of equal rights deepened, he made a strong commitment to the cause and continued to work for justice. Now Martin and Bobby were both speaking out about the need to address poverty and income inequality and demanding an end to the unjust war in Vietnam.

10:00 AM (EST)
The White House, Washington, DC
While Martin flew to Memphis, Bobby Kennedy arrived for his meeting with President Johnson. It would be the first conversation they'd had since LBJ's surprising speech three days earlier when he'd announced that he would not seek another term as president. Johnson's back was against the wall. Only 26 percent of Americans approved of his handling of the war. During his television address Johnson had declared that he would suspend bombing raids against North Vietnam and seek a peaceful settlement to end the war, measures that both Bobby and Martin had been publicly demanding for many months.

Still, Bobby was shocked that Johnson had withdrawn from the race. He'd anguished over whether to run against Johnson because of the war. Bobby didn't want to tear apart the Democratic Party by competing against a sitting president, and he worried about the toll a national campaign would take on his wife, Ethel, and their 10 children. In 1967, as Johnson continued to escalate the number of troops serving in Vietnam, political activist Allard Low-enstein had begged Bobby to run as the party's antiwar candidate. The country could not survive four more years of an unjust war, Allard told him.

When Bobby decided he would wait until 1972 to run for president, after Johnson's second term, Allard was furious. The "Dump Johnson" movement would find someone else to run, he said, someone like Martin Luther King. Martin declined. But in November 1967, Senator Eugene McCarthy of Minnesota declared his candidacy.

A month before, the Kerner Commission, appointed by President Johnson to investigate the causes of the riots in poor city neighborhoods, had issued a strongly worded report: "Our nation is moving toward two societies, one black, one white—separate and unequal. . . . It is time to make good the promises of American democracy to all citizens—urban and rural, white and black." The bipartisan commission of both Republican and Democratic officials offered many solutions, including job creation, better housing options, and training for police in race relations, similar to what both Martin and Bobby had been advocating since 1965.

When the president made no public statement about implementing suggestions from the report and continued to intensify war efforts, Bobby reached a breaking point. He had tried reasoning with Johnson in private and tried pressuring him in public. Now only one route remained. He had to make his voice heard, whether it was too late or not.

Knowing he'd never be happy if he didn't try to run for president, Ethel Kennedy convinced her husband to declare his candidacy, and on March 16, 1968, he finally did. Bobby knew he had no guarantee of victory. Eighty percent of Americans still supported the war and did not approve of his views. He had a big job ahead to energize black voters and win back the young antiwar Democrats who currently backed McCarthy.

Before his first campaign appearance on March 18 at the University of Kansas, Bobby had worried about turnout and the reception to his straight talk about addressing poverty and ending the war. As he began to speak, his hands shook and his voice was tentative. But as the cheers grew in volume, he grew more confident, urging the students to get involved and hold elected officials accountable, especially about the Vietnam War. He admitted that he had been involved in his brother's decision to help fight Communism by sending 15,000 military advisors to South Vietnam in 1961. But seven years later troop levels had reached 500,000 with no end to the conflict in sight.

"This country needs honesty and candor in its political life and from the president of the United States," Bobby said. "I want us to find out the promise of the future, what we can accomplish here in the United States, what this country does stand for and what is expected of us in the years ahead."

He talked about the need to help Americans who go to bed hungry every night. Then he described another kind of poverty: "a poverty of satisfaction—a lack of purpose

Wherever Bobby campaigned, people reached out to touch him and make a connection, as on this day in Detroit, Michigan.

and dignity—that inflicts us all." Bobby had been raised in a very wealthy family, but he had also learned that the accumulation of material things could not make a person happy. His sincerity and connection to the audience convinced the students that this was true.

Bobby ended his speech with a heartfelt plea: "I don't think that we have to shoot each other, to beat each other, to curse each other and criticize each other, I think that we can do better in this country. And that is why I run for president of the United States."

After Kansas, he traveled the country for two weeks, visiting 30 states, bringing his ideas directly to the people rather than depending on press interviews and campaign ads. He didn't offer easy solutions or slogans to win votes. Bobby told Americans not only what was wrong with the country but also how they could help. He continued to challenge his listeners to do more for others, to reach out to those less fortunate.

Then on March 31 everything changed. Johnson was out of the race. The Democratic nomination was wide open.

During their meeting that morning of April 3, Bobby told Johnson that he understood the difficulties and burdens borne by the president. Bobby had been his brother's closest adviser for three years and knew well the challenges of the presidency and the loneliness of leading the country.

Johnson told Bobby that he'd been loyal to JFK's policies, but young people and black voters had turned against him. "I want everybody to get together to find a way to stop the killing." Bobby could not have agreed more. The war in Vietnam must end.

After Johnson promised to honor his neutrality pledge, by not publicly supporting any of the Democratic candidates, Bobby left the White House feeling optimistic. The next day he was headed to Indiana to compete in his first presidential primary, ready to fight for the Democratic nomination and win.

2

"I'VE BEEN TO THE MOUNTAINTOP"

April 3, 1968

Memphis, Tennessee

Martin's 30-minute flight landed just ahead of the bad weather. On the ground, SCLC associates Andrew Young, James Bevel, Jesse Jackson, and Hosea Williams had to tell "Doc" the disappointing news: that morning the Memphis mayor had obtained a federal court order preventing Monday's march. It was another setback, Martin told them, but they couldn't give up. The dignity of all workers mattered, and all workers deserved fair pay. They would just have to convince the judge to overturn the ruling.

Martin and Ralph drove to the Lorraine Motel and checked in. All the motel rooms opened onto a balcony, so the security was not ideal. But Martin liked supporting the black business owner, who made sure his favorite room was always available. As Martin stood on the balcony outside room 306, US marshals arrived and served him with a federal injunction stopping Monday's march. Martin informed the gathered reporters that he and the SCLC would ask the judge to withdraw his mandate against the march. He never liked to violate a federal order, he told them. But the workers deserved their support, and, as Americans, the marchers had the right of free speech. If necessary, they would defy the court ruling and march on Monday.

Later that day, Martin and Ralph sat in Martin's room, reminiscing about Martin's childhood and family life, their long friendship, and their many days in jail together—for the cause. Ralph understood that this was Martin's way of relaxing since his friend never talked directly about the pressure he was under.

At 4:30 PM Martin felt under the weather and lay down to rest. As he slept, lightning flashed in the sky and the wind whipped against the window. When he awoke later, Ralph told him about the huge storm, a twister that had hit north of town. Martin still didn't feel well, and the storm would likely mean a small turnout at the rally that night. The press would call it another one of his failures. He begged Ralph to go in his place.

7:30 PM (CST)

When Ralph, James, Jesse, Hosea, and Andrew arrived at Mason Temple, supporters waited in the pews in spite of the tornado warning and gale winds outside. It wasn't a huge crowd like on March 18 when Martin spoke to 15,000

supporters of the strike. But tonight 2,000 sanitation workers, friends, and family had braved the storm to hear their
leader.

When Johnnie Turner Rogers heard that Dr. King
would be speaking that night, she didn't worry about the
weather. Her only thought was *How quickly can I get there?*
Johnnie had been an activist since her college days and

Martin and Ralph being arrested in Birmingham, Alabama, in May
1963. Over the years they had been jailed more than 40 times.

never missed a chance to hear Martin speak. She had traveled to Washington, DC, for the 1963 March on Washington and heard Martin tell about his dream.

On March 18 she'd crowded into this very church, listening as he told the cheering crowd that they had come together to demand that the city of Memphis honor the dignity of workers. *"You are demonstrating that we can stick together. You are demonstrating that we are all tied in a single garment of destiny, and that if one black person suffers, if one black person is down, we are all down."*

Sanitation worker Taylor Rogers had come tonight with his wife, Betty. He knew that Dr. King had put everything aside to come to Memphis to support them, the workers on the bottom of the ladder who were paid so little.

Willie Wilbert Herenton was also in the audience. He had heard Martin speak on March 18 too. Over the years, he'd listened to Martin's recorded speeches over and over. Without the insights and inspiration of Dr. King, he never would have gained the confidence to become one of the few black administrators in the Memphis school district.

Ralph studied the crowd. A local preacher spoke from the pulpit, but people kept looking around for a sign of their beloved Dr. King. Outside, sirens blared, sheets of rain poured down, thunder rumbled, and lightning filled the sky. Martin must preach, thought Ralph. People had faced a hellish night to get here and deserved no less.

Ralph rushed into the vestibule and called his friend on the telephone. "Martin, the people who are here want you, not me. All the television networks are lined up with their

cameras, waiting for you." They both knew how important press coverage was to their cause.

9:00 PM

The crowd exploded when they caught sight of Martin
walking up the aisle. Ralph rushed up to the pulpit. Usually Martin spoke first, and then Ralph covered the logistics for the upcoming protest. But this night Ralph wanted
to go first, though later he couldn't explain why. He talked
for 30 minutes about Martin's storied life, his awards and
accomplishments, and the history of their long friendship.

Ralph told the crowd that Martin had not yet decided
whether to run for president of the United States, "but
he is the one who tells the president what to do." Ralph's
tone was joking, but in a way his words were true. Martin
would certainly influence the next president, especially if
Robert Kennedy won the election.

When Martin took the podium at 9:30 PM, his slow,
lilting voice competed with the raging storm outside. He
thanked his best friend Ralph and then the crowd for coming out in such inclement weather. With no notes to follow
and still not feeling well, he stumbled at first, distracted
by the shutters hitting against the temple walls, until the
Reverend Billy Kyles found a custodian to stop the noise.
Only then, at the crowd's urging, did Martin's words begin
to pour out.

He told them that he was upset the media had focused
only on the violence of last week's protest and not on the
work conditions of the 1,300 sanitation workers. He urged

the people gathered to support the workers and march on Monday. "We aren't going to let dogs or water hoses turn us around. We aren't going to let any injunction turn us around."

The people cheered, remembering how the children of Birmingham, Alabama, had not stopped marching in 1963, even when fire hoses and vicious dogs were set upon them by the racist commissioner of safety Bull Connor, just for standing up against segregation.

Martin told the crowd about the girl from New York who wrote him a letter in 1958 after he was stabbed in the chest with a letter opener at a signing in Harlem for his first book, *Stride Toward Freedom*, about the Montgomery bus boycott. The tip of the blade had come so close to his aorta that a sneeze would have killed him.

If he had sneezed, he wouldn't have been around for the lunch counter protests when college students silently sat

> *"Dear Dr. King, I am a ninth-grade student at the White Plains High School. While it should not matter, I would like to mention that I'm a white girl. I read in the paper of your misfortune, and of your suffering. And I read that if you had sneezed, you would have died. And I'm simply writing you to say that I'm so happy that you didn't sneeze."*
> —Author unknown

down to protest the segregation of white only restaurants. Or the Freedom Rides, when white and black Americans rode together throughout the South to protest segregated seating on buses and in waiting rooms. He wouldn't have been around to tell the country about his dream, or when black people aroused the conscience of Americans by their protests or when Americans, white and black, demanded that Congress pass the Civil Rights Act. Martin wouldn't have been around for the voting march in Selma or tonight in Memphis to rally around the workers.

As he came to the end of his speech he said, "We've got some difficult days ahead. But it really doesn't matter with me now, because I've been to the mountaintop. . . . I've seen the Promised Land."

Over the years Martin had often compared the struggle for racial equality to reaching the Promised Land. He told how in the biblical story in the book of Exodus the Egyptians enslaved the Israelites, but through the leadership of Moses and the guidance of God, they gained freedom from their captors. The Exodus story had long inspired black people to continue their fight against injustice.

"I may not get there with you," Martin said. "But I want you to know tonight that we, as a people, will get to the Promised Land."

Willie Wilbert Herenton watched as tears rolled down Dr. King's cheeks and an almost "supernatural glow" surrounded his face.

"Yes!" the crowd cried, rising to its feet. By now, everyone was crying, even the cameramen. Andrew Young wondered how Doc could end such an emotional speech. But then Martin began to say the words to his favorite hymn, "Mine eyes have seen the glory of the coming of the Lord . . ."

Wheeling around, an exhausted Martin slumped into Ralph's arms. Jesse Jackson jumped up from the front pew to help Doc to his seat as people swarmed the altar, reaching out, straining to touch their hero.

3

"WHAT WE REALLY STAND FOR"

Thursday, April 4, 1968, noon (EST)
South Bend, Indiana
Cheering high school students lined the route as Bobby left the airport in a red convertible and headed to the University of Notre Dame. As he leaned out of the back seat, waving to the crowd, enthusiastic teens ran into the street, hoping to shake his hand.

At Notre Dame 5,000 students crammed into the Stepan Center, while hundreds more stood outside. "This is the most affluent nation the world has ever known," Bobby shouted to the crowd. "If we cannot prevent our fellow citizens from starving, we must ask ourselves what kind of country we really are; we must ask ourselves what we really stand for."

Since Bobby's 1964 election as senator from New York, he'd made countless trips around the country. Visiting urban neighborhoods, American Indian reservations, and

California farmworkers on strike, he'd been touched by the problems of all the people he met. He'd been especially affected by his trip the year before to the Mississippi delta, one of the poorest parts of the United States, where starving children with bloated stomachs and sores on their skin had brought him to tears. He returned to Washington determined to do something about poverty.

That night he burst into the kitchen where his children were eating dinner. He stood in silence and then said, "I've just come from a part of the country where three families have to live in a room this size. You've *got* to help those children," Bobby told his family. *"Please* help those children." He repeated it three times, his seventh child, Kerry Kennedy, said years later.

At Notre Dame he told the students that the government didn't have all the solutions and that poverty programs are most successful when informed by the voices of poor people themselves. That's why he had contacted Dr. King a year ago, encouraging the idea of bringing poor people to Washington, DC, to meet with government officials. Now the Poor People's Campaign was about to start.

After his speech Bobby stopped at St. Joseph's County Home for the Aged. He visited children wherever he went, but he also had a soft spot for older citizens, perhaps because of his father back home in Massachusetts. Felled by a stroke in 1961, the powerful Joseph Kennedy Sr. had been unable to speak ever since.

Bobby quietly answered the residents' questions about Medicare and Social Security. Then he told them, "If this

country amounts to anything now, it's because of what
you have done."

At the South Bend airport, Bobby and a few of his advisors headed out on a smaller plane for Muncie, Indiana, while the rest of the team flew to Indianapolis to prepare for the evening events.

Noon (CST)
Memphis, Tennessee
In Memphis, Jim Bevel led a training session on nonviolence, preparing local teens for a peaceful march on Monday. Jim had trained thousands of young people over the years, notably those who marched so bravely against segregation in 1963 in Birmingham. That morning Dr. King's trusted adviser Andy Young testified in court on behalf of the SCLC, trying to persuade the judge that they could guarantee a peaceful protest on Monday.

Martin shared a fried catfish meal with Ralph and anxiously awaited word about the hearing. After lunch he led a planning meeting for the upcoming Poor People's Campaign. On April 22, 3,000 volunteers from many groups—American Indian tribal members, Hispanics, poor whites, young black gang members, and farmworkers—would depart in caravans from 10 cities and 5 rural areas and meet in the nation's capital.

3:00 PM (CST)
When Martin's younger brother A.D. arrived from Louisville, Kentucky, the two men called their parents, talking

and laughing with them for over an hour. "She's always happy when A.D.'s with me," Martin told Ralph afterward. "[Mother] doesn't often have a chance to talk to us both together."

Andy returned from court at 5:00 PM. The judge had listened to his plea that Dr. King and the SCLC were the last supporters of nonviolence and overturned the injunction. Monday's march could proceed if weapons were outlawed and participants walked in narrow ranks on a prescribed course, so federal marshals could line the route. Guns had never been allowed during marches. Martin had given up his own weapon years before during the Montgomery bus boycott.

Pleased about the decision, Doc wrestled Andy to the floor and started tickling him, teasing him for not reporting in earlier. A.D., Ralph, and Hosea began attacking Andy with pillows. It was a free-for-all. Andy had not seen Doc this relaxed in months.

6:00 PM (EST)
Muncie, Indiana
Bobby stood on a stage at Ball State University and shouted to the huge crowd gathered in the field house. "Indiana, are you ready to help elect a president?"

"Bobby! Bobby! Bobby!" the students cried, cheering and clapping.

A savvy politician, Bobby first told a few jokes and complimented the local officials sitting on the stage. But then he got serious. Again he talked about Americans' personal responsibility to help poor people in the country: "Here in America there are children so underfed and so undernourished, that many of them are crippled for life in mind and body before the age of three."

His demanding message challenged the students to think about other people. Still the audience cheered. If a wealthy Kennedy understood the needs of the disadvantaged, then maybe they should too.

Bobby told them that the 1968 election would determine the direction the United States would move in, and urged, "The American people should examine everything. Not take anything for granted. Americans have a moral obligation and should make an honest effort to understand one another and move forward together." He was talking about the Vietnam War, poverty, riots, and police violence. Like Martin, he wanted everyone to get involved and help solve these problems.

After his speech, Bobby answered questions for 30 minutes. He never gave canned responses or campaign slogans. He loved the give-and-take of these sessions and learning about the concerns of real people. When a skeptical student accused him of double-talking without promising any specific solutions, the crowd erupted in boos.

But Bobby wasn't frustrated by the comment. "He's perfectly entitled to disagree with me," he told the students. "That's the only way we're going to make progress in this country—if people stand up and speak their minds."

One of the few black students in the auditorium shouted out the final question. "Your speech implies that you are

Martin stands on the balcony of the Lorraine Motel the day before he was assassinated, with SCLC associates (from left) Hosea Williams, Jesse Jackson, and Ralph Abernathy.

placing a great deal of faith in white America. Is that faith justified?"

"Yes. Faith in black America is justified, too." Bobby hesitated. "Although there are extremists on both sides . . . the vast majority of the American people want to do the decent and right thing here within our country."

After the questions, a surge of young people stormed the platform, reaching out to shake hands with Bobby and his wife, Ethel. Two press tables were toppled, and three students were injured in the stampede. Bobby was mobbed after every speech, and his campaign workers were concerned for his safety. But Bobby seemed to feed off the frenzy, drawing energy from the enthusiasm. He knew that there were dangerous people out there. But he refused to use security guards. They made him feel penned in.

5:45 PM (CST)
Memphis, Tennessee
Martin returned to his motel room to get ready for dinner. In the room below, Jesse Jackson rehearsed freedom songs with the band performing at the rally that night. By 6:00 PM, Jim Bevel, Jesse, and others had gathered in the courtyard. Jesse called up to Martin, who stood on the balcony. "Doc, you remember Ben Branch?"

"How are you, Ben?" Martin asked. "Ben, make sure you play 'Precious Lord, Take My Hand' at the meeting tonight. Play it real pretty."

Jim Bevel was just about to holler up to tell Doc about the enthusiastic young people at the training that day, when a single shot punctured the air.

4

"WHEN IS THIS VIOLENCE GOING TO STOP?"

7:00 PM (EST)

Indianapolis, Indiana

Hundreds of supporters had lined up on an empty lot surrounded by trees next to the Broadway Christian Center on 18th and Broadway, excited to meet President Kennedy's brother, the man who might be the next president. Every home in the neighborhood had photos of Dr. King and President Kennedy hanging on the wall.

The people in the crowd didn't know that Senator Kennedy was running behind schedule and hadn't even left Muncie yet. But it wouldn't have mattered. Even though the weather was cool and overcast, people were upbeat, enjoying the rock music booming through the loudspeakers. Campaign worker John Lewis surveyed the mostly black crowd, most of whom lived in the neighborhood. White supporters from other parts of town had arrived early and lined up in front.

John had joined the Kennedy campaign just a few days earlier, the first black civil rights leader to sign on. He had worked for equal rights since he was 15, when he'd heard Dr. King speak on the radio during the Montgomery bus boycott. Since 1955 he'd helped organize the student sit-ins, been beaten up during the Freedom Rides, and represented the Student Nonviolent Coordinating Committee as the youngest speaker at the March on Washington. He had almost died in 1965 when he was attacked by the state police after leading 800 protestors onto the Edmund Pettus Bridge in Selma, Alabama.

Now, after all the violence and upheaval of three summers of rioting, John believed that Senator Kennedy was the only presidential candidate at this time who could bring the country together and bridge the gap between rich and poor, black and white. He had watched the senator change since his early days as attorney general, when he and President Kennedy hadn't yet understood injustice against black Americans.

John was determined to help the senator win the Indiana primary on May 7. His job was to rally Bobby's black supporters. That's why he'd helped select this site for Bobby's first campaign speech in Indianapolis and had set up tables to register new voters. The committee had also chosen this location to highlight problems with local police. Many felt that the officers treated black people in the neighborhood differently than they treated white people in white neighborhoods.

Two months earlier, the white store owner of nearby Light's Market had shot a young black man, 15-year-old Peter Bible, in the arm with a .38-caliber rifle—without cause. After the shooting, one policeman reportedly told Bible, "You ought to be dead." Bible and his older brother were tried in juvenile court for disorderly conduct and assault and battery. The charges were dropped against the boys, but none were filed against Alvis Light.

Civil rights activists demanded an investigation by the Board of Public Safety. But police still did not charge Light.

Snooky Hendricks, head of the local Black Action Project, organized a boycott against shopping at the store. Outside, marchers carried signs that read LET'S SEND LIGHT BACK TO THE WHITES. Still there was no action. Many protestors thought it was because Light had a son on the police force.

Organizers hoped that Bobby's appearance at the rally that night would send a message to the Indianapolis mayor that something must be done about Alvis Light.

Kennedy supporter and labor union organizer Jim Trulock had arrived early to help community activist Ben Bell set up a stage on the back of a truck trailer. Afterward Jim passed out KENNEDY signs to the gathering crowd, while Ben distributed brochures with information about the nearby College Room, a community center for young people, where he served as director. The College Room offered programs on how to stay in school, stay out of jail, and work for change in the city.

Loraine Minor and her friend Patricia Parr stood near the trees. They had walked over from school and were the first teens to arrive. The two girls were excited to have a real senator come to their park and anxious to hear what Kennedy had to say. Loraine's boyfriend, Gene, was serving in Vietnam, but his letters never talked about what he was going through. Dr. King and Senator Kennedy had both spoken out against the war. What did Gene think about it, Loraine wondered?

Eight-year-old Mark Higbee waited next to his father. He had begged his dad to come, even though it was a school night. A week before, they'd helped stuff envelopes at the Kennedy campaign headquarters downtown. Mark hoped he'd get to shake Bobby's hand since there were only a few kids in the crowd.

Sixteen-year-old Altha Cravey and her friend Mary Evans stood shoulder to shoulder in the packed crowd. Mary was white and had never seen so many black people. The only black person she knew was her family's maid. Her parents were loyal Republicans.

Both girls supported Democratic candidate Senator Eugene McCarthy because he had been the first candidate to speak out against the Vietnam War. But they wanted to hear what Bobby had to say.

Altha's father made the girls move over near the sidewalk, for a quick escape if the crowd started rioting. The night before, Altha and her dad had a big fight about her attendance at an event in this part of town. Raised in the rural South, Mr. Cravey had been taught that black people

> *"Civil rights leader Dr. Martin Luther King Jr. was shot at a downtown Memphis hotel shortly before 7 PM EST this evening."* —CBS Radio

were dangerous and not to be trusted. But when Altha insisted on going, her dad drove the girls to make sure they were safe.

Ben Bell's wife, JoMarva, and daughter, India, sat on their front porch, listening to the radio and watching the crowd gather across the street. It was India's 13th birthday, but they had postponed her party because of Senator Kennedy's speech that night. Suddenly, a special report interrupted the music.

JoMarva listened just long enough to learn that a white male had been spotted fleeing the Memphis hotel, and then she rushed across the street to find her husband. She had to tell him before people in the crowd found out and something awful happened. It was still light out when she whispered the horrible news to Ben and Jim Trulock. Ben began putting away the tables covered with brochures and voting materials. Jim became nervous for Bobby Kennedy, and for all of them.

Walter Sheridan, head of the statewide Kennedy campaign, located John Lewis. "We just got word that Dr. King has been shot in Memphis."

John couldn't think. He couldn't talk. Dr. King meant everything to him. But Martin would pull through. He always did. He had to.

John looked around. People were still talking and clapping to the music. They didn't seem to know yet.

When Mayor Richard Lugar received the news that Martin had been shot, he called Kennedy campaign organizer Mike Riley, demanding that the campaign cancel the rally. His police could not guarantee the senator's safety. When Mike said that Bobby was coming anyway, the mayor threatened to block off the streets with fire trucks since it was against the law to drive over fire hoses.

"Then they'll walk if they have to," Mike responded.

7:30 PM (CST)

At the Muncie airport Bobby and Ethel shook hands with supporters lining the fence along the runway. As they headed to the plane, a black teen called out, "Have you heard about Martin Luther King?"

Bobby swiveled around. "Was he shot?" Ever since his brother's death, shootings were never far from his mind.

The young man nodded. "He's in critical condition."

Bobby shook his head and walked up the steps to the plane. Inside, when a campaign worker confirmed the news about King, Bobby's body "sagged" and "his eyes went blank," as if the reality of Martin's shooting had finally registered.

Recalling his statement at Ball State, he said, "To think that I just finished saying that white America wants to do

the right thing, and even while I was talking this happened
. . . all this divisiveness, all this hate. We have to do something about the divisions and the hate."

As the airplane taxied down the runway, Bobby asked
his press secretary, Frank Mankiewicz, what he should
say at the rally in Indianapolis. "Give a very short speech,"
Frank advised. "It should almost be a prayer."

Then Bobby sat alone, staring out the window during
the 30-minute flight. Perhaps he thought about the agoniz-
ing 30 minutes he had waited for word about his brother's
condition after the president had been shot in Dallas in
1963; near the end of the trip, he turned to reporter John
Lindsay of *Newsweek* magazine and said, "I know what
Mrs. King and her children are going through."

7:00 PM (CST)
Memphis
"He's going," the doctor said to Ralph Abernathy. "If you'd
like to spend a few last moments with him, you can have
them now."

Ralph took Martin into his arms and held him as his
friend's breaths came farther and farther apart.

**"Dr. Martin Luther King Jr, Nobel Peace Prize win-
ner, has died in Memphis, Tennessee."**
—WCCO Radio

When Coretta had learned about her husband's shooting, she rushed to the Atlanta airport to catch a flight to Memphis. But when she arrived and heard that Martin was gone, she returned home to her children. Her place was with them, she told a friend.

Willie Wilbert Herenton heard the news on WDIA, Memphis's black radio station, while driving home in the car. A deep sorrow overwhelmed him. His hero was gone.

He would never forget the halo of light surrounding Dr. King's head the night before.

8:30 PM (EST)
Indianapolis
When Bobby's plane landed, a campaign worker turned on the radio. When they heard the news that Martin had died, reporter John Lindsay watched Bobby shrink back, as though struck physically. Then Bobby put his face in his hands and said, "Oh, God. When is this violence going to stop?"

5

"TO WHOM MUCH IS GIVEN, MUCH IS ASKED"

Bobby Kennedy was never destined to be the Kennedy son who ran for president. The responsibility to fulfill their father's dream of a son in the White House belonged to the eldest, Joe Jr. As the shy third son, Bobby's role was to support his older brothers in their many endeavors. All the Kennedy children grew up with the motto FAMILY FIRST.

Born in 1925, the seventh of nine children, Bobby grew up with every privilege that wealth offered. His father, Joseph, was a brilliant businessman. Though he'd grown up in a poor immigrant family, Joseph made millions by acquiring businesses and producing movies. His money helped him overcome the prejudice against Irish Catholics at that time and allowed his children to attend the best private schools and travel the world. His wealth bought him political privilege too. In 1938, President Franklin Delano Roosevelt appointed Joseph ambassador to Great

Britain. The family lived in England in the years before World War II.

Bobby admired his handsome, smart older brothers, John (whom the family called Jack) and Joe Jr., and wanted

The Kennedy children at their summer home in Hyannis Port, Massachusetts. Left to right: Jean, Bobby, Patricia, Eunice, Kathleen, Rosemary, Jack, and Joe Jr.

to be just like them. But because he was years younger, he usually took his place among his sisters, often cowering upstairs when Joe Jr. and Jack wrestled downstairs.

"We don't want any losers around here," their father often instructed the children. "Don't come in second or third. Win." In his mind, the biggest victory would be if Joe Jr. were elected president of the United States, to show that an Irish Catholic could become the most powerful person in the world. Joseph prepared all his sons and daughters for a public life by conducting nightly current events lessons around the dinner table. Their mother, Rose, watched over their spiritual life, taking the children to Catholic mass and praying the rosary with them every evening.

Both parents emphasized a duty to service, stressing that "to whom much is given, much is asked," as Jesus said in the Gospel according to Luke. Even though the Kennedys had wealth and privilege, the children were taught to help others too. More than either of his older brothers, Bobby shared his mother's deep Catholic faith, often serving as an altar boy at daily mass. This spirituality developed in his childhood later sustained him through many challenging times as an adult.

As a boy, Bobby didn't feel like a winner. He always seemed to be trying to prove his courage and striving harder than anyone else. In high school at Milton Academy, he was still quiet and shy. He lacked his brother Jack's easy confidence and often brooded about things—but not on the football field. "Attacking the game as if it were some sort of moral test, Bobby ran every practice play, and tackled and blocked dummies as if he were in a hard fought game," his friend Sam Adams remembered.

"He didn't care about fitting in and going along with the crowd. A guy would tell a dirty joke, and Bobby wouldn't laugh . . . said there were more important things to talk about, and he'd turn his back and walk away," Adams explained. Bobby spent his time thinking about current events and problems in the world.

In 1943, six weeks before his 18th birthday, Bobby enlisted in the United States Naval Reserve. In the spring of 1944 he left Milton Academy before graduation to report to the V-12 Navy College Training Program at Harvard College. But World War II ended before Bobby saw any military action.

Jack and Joe Jr. had earlier joined the US Navy. Jack became a war hero when he rescued his crewmen after their PT 109 boat was destroyed by the Japanese. Joe Jr. was a hero, too, flying 35 bombing missions for the Allied Forces. But he was killed during a secret bombing raid over France when his plane exploded in midair. The family was devastated, especially Bobby.

But the Kennedys were raised to soldier on and to help fulfill their father's wish—a son in the White House. Jack had dreamed of becoming a journalist or college professor after the war, but as the next in line, he took Joe Jr.'s place. The first stop was the 1946 campaign for a seat in Congress.

Jack didn't expect much help from his moody younger brother, who lacked social skills. But Bobby turned out to be an excellent campaigner. Elections suited Bobby. "They were like sports—a great game with an enemy to defeat and a victory to be won," wrote Bobby's biographer Marc Aronson. "They were like religion—a ritual in which he could organize the faithful and fight for good."

When his big brother won the election, all was right in Bobby's world.

Though his high school grades had been only average, his father's money and influence got Bobby admitted to Harvard College in the fall of 1946. His father and Joe Jr. and Jack had also attended Harvard, the top college in the country.

Bobby's grades remained mediocre in college, but he accomplished something his two older brothers and father never did. He won a Harvard varsity letter in football, even though early in his senior season he'd broken his leg. The coach was so impressed by the fact that Bobby kept practicing with a cast on his leg that he let him start in the final game of the season.

That year Bobby also began to show support for racial equality. He hadn't grown up around black people, so he didn't understand the racism they experienced every day. He did understand the need for justice and fairness, having listened to his father's stories about how Irish Catholic immigrants were considered second-class citizens when they moved to America. They had trouble getting decent jobs to support a family and had to live in the poorer areas of town.

When the Harvard football team traveled to the University of Virginia in the fall of 1948, the team's only black player, Chester Pierce, was informed that he could not room with the other players or play in the game. Even though the year before Jackie Robinson had broken the color line in Major League Baseball, becoming the first African American to play in the league, black people, even famous athletes, were not allowed to stay in the same places as white people. Bobby convinced the rest of the Harvard players to boycott the game unless Pierce was allowed to sleep in the dorm with them and play the next day. Not wanting to cancel their homecoming game, University of Virginia officials reluctantly relented. Pierce became the first colored football player to play against a white team in the South.

After graduating from Harvard, Bobby attended law school at the University of Virginia. In 1951 he led another protest against segregation. During his third year, as president of the Student League Forum, Bobby invited Dr. Ralph Bunche, the first black winner of the Nobel Peace Prize, to speak on campus, even though he knew that Virginia law still forbade the mingling of blacks and whites in public places. Bunche accepted the invitation, but only if he could present before a racially integrated audience.

Bobby lobbied university administrators to allow both white and black people to attend the lecture. They reluctantly agreed, citing a Supreme Court ruling that banned segregation in higher education. Bobby was happy about the victory, but he didn't understand why the law students from the South were unwilling to stand with him. It would take another 12 years for Bobby to comprehend that many white Southerners and other white Americans, too, didn't want to give up the privilege, their favored status as white people, that they had grown up with. These early protests taught Bobby how to hold his ground in a moral fight.

———— ★ ————

Martin Luther King Jr. grew up in a very different world than the Kennedys. Two years younger than Bobby, Martin, called M.L. or Mike as a boy, was born in 1929 to a middle-class family. He and his two siblings lived in a comfortable home with supportive parents who believed in the importance of education. But Martin was black and lived in Atlanta, Georgia, where segregation laws prevented him from playing in the same parks, attending the same schools, and shopping in the same stores as white children.

Martin's parents encouraged him not to hate white people and to believe in his own self-worth. But they couldn't shield him from the pain of racial segregation, especially when he lost his best friend at age six because the boy's father refused to allow his son to play with black children.

Martin and his older sister, Christine, and younger brother, A.D., found a second home at Ebenezer Baptist Church. Every Sunday they listened to their father's sermons urging people to stand up for equal rights. Dr. King Sr. preached that an unjust human law like segregation is contrary to God's moral law. Therefore, people had a duty to oppose it. As he grew older, Martin came to understand what his father meant.

When Martin was 11, a white woman slapped his face because he accidentally stepped on her foot. Martin learned how to handle his anger over such treatment by watching his father. One time when a white shoe clerk insisted that Martin and his father move to the back of the line in order to be served, Daddy King marched out of the store instead. When a policeman pulled over his father's car and called him "boy" when asking to see his driver's license, Daddy King pointed to Martin. "This is a boy, I'm a man; until you call me one, I will not listen to you."

His father refused to ride the streetcar because black passengers had to sit in the back.

Martin's parents were active members of the National Association for the Advancement of Colored People. The NAACP was America's oldest and largest organization fighting against racial discrimination. The King family boycotted the movie theaters where black people had to sit in a separate section and lunch counters where they couldn't buy a cup of coffee just because of their skin color. These Jim Crow laws were local ordinances in Southern states that mandated segregated schools, restaurants, transportation, and other public facilities by race.

Martin was a talented boy, good at many things. He especially liked public speaking and often practiced in front of a mirror, "believing that if you had the right set of words, you could move the world." Family friends sensed that young Martin had a gift for oratory and would do something special in his life.

At Booker T. Washington High School he played football, sang in the glee club, and excelled in debate and speech. In April 1944 the Colored Elks Clubs of Georgia sponsored a contest at their state convention. Fifteen-year-old Martin won the contest with a speech he wrote himself. In "The Negro and the Constitution" he contrasted the promises of President Lincoln's 1863 Emancipation Proclamation that freed slaves in the Confederacy with the current segregation laws in the South that served as another form of slavery: "My heart throbs anew in the hope that inspired by the example of Lincoln, imbued with the spirit of Christ, [America] will cast down the last barrier to perfect freedom."

He faced such a barrier on the bus trip home from the contest, when the driver ordered Martin and another student to surrender their seats to a white couple. Even when the driver cursed at them, the two teenagers remained in their seats until their teacher persuaded them to move. "It was the angriest I have ever been," Martin later said.

In the fall of 1944 Morehouse College in Atlanta invited high school students to enroll at their college. Attendance had dropped because many young men were away fighting in World War II. Martin passed the entrance exam and at age 15 was admitted to his father's alma mater. He joined an interracial league with students from other local colleges and was happy to learn that some white people cared about ending segregation too.

Martin wasn't sure he wanted to be a minister like his father and grandfather and considered studying law

Martin, pictured third from left, attending a lecture at Morehouse College in 1948.

or medicine. But during his last year, Martin decided the social gospel of the Christian church offered the best way to fight for justice. He was especially influenced by Benjamin Mays, president of Morehouse College, who first introduced Martin to Mohandas Gandhi's nonviolent resistance movement. Martin was intrigued by Gandhi's use of marches, boycotts, and other nonviolent protests to successfully lead India's movement for independence against Great Britain.

6

"UNTIL JUSTICE RUNS DOWN LIKE WATER"

In 1948, after graduating from Morehouse College, Martin enrolled at Crozier Theological Seminary in Chester, Pennsylvania. It was the first time he lived in the North and attended classes with white students. At Crozier he began a quest to discover how to eliminate segregation.

After three years of earning outstanding grades and excelling in student leadership, he was awarded a scholarship to study for a doctorate in theology. At Boston University, through his intellectual and spiritual readings, Martin came to believe that the evil of segregation could be offset by the power of Christian love and nonviolent resistance.

Martin finished his coursework in 1953 and married Coretta Scott, a vocalist studying music in Boston who had grown up in Alabama. The couple decided to return to the South, where they believed they could better serve in ministry and work to end segregation. In spite of his father's wishes that he return to Atlanta, Martin accepted a pastorship at Dexter Avenue Baptist Church in Montgomery, Alabama. His eloquent speaking style and thoughtful sermons about equal rights both challenged and pleased his new congregation.

Martin's life changed forever on December 1, 1955. Rosa Parks, secretary of the NAACP's Montgomery, Alabama, branch, refused to surrender her seat on the bus to a white man and was arrested for violating a local segregation law. The following Monday, a group of black clergymen and community leaders encouraged a one-day boycott of the buses. It was so successful that the leaders formed the Montgomery Improvement Association to continue the protest. Just the year before, the US Supreme Court had declared that state laws establishing separate public schools for black and white students were unconstitutional in the landmark case *Brown v. Board of Education*. The boycott leaders also believed it was unconstitutional for people of color to have to sit in the back of the bus or give up their seat to a white person.

The new organization needed a strong leader to encourage the black people of Montgomery to continue the protest. The leaders were divided on whom that should be. A newcomer in town, Martin was startled when he was nominated for the position. But his inspirational speaking style and openness to all groups made him an excellent choice, and the vote was unanimous. When asked if he would accept the position, he said, "If I can be of service."

Rev. Ralph Abernathy was named the coordinator of logistics, directing the day-to-day operation of the boycott.

Martin rushed home to prepare his speech for the rally that evening. He would have to convince black residents who had been mistreated and discriminated against by white people all their lives that nonviolent resistance would earn them a seat at the front of the bus. He hesitated to tell Coretta about his new role. It would mean even more time away from her and their baby, Yolanda. But he needn't have worried. She wholeheartedly supported him and the boycott.

Martin arrived at the Holt Street Baptist Church with only a few notes on paper, nothing like his usual 15-hour preparation for a Sunday sermon. Hundreds of anxious supporters packed the pews, while another thousand stood outside. For years Martin had studied the moral and legal reasons why they had a right to protest. But when he told the crowd that the US Constitution guaranteed them this right, they were still restless and nervous. It was a huge risk to protest against the segregation law and white people in power. They could lose their jobs.

He did not yet have their trust because many of them did not know this young minister. Still they kept listening. And by the time he called out, "We are determined here in Montgomery to work and fight until justice runs down like water, and righteousness like a mighty stream," his thundering baritone had moved their hearts. When he shouted that the only weapon they had was the weapon of nonviolent protest, that they would attack the system but not the individuals who perpetuated it, they stood up and cheered.

They would not ride the bus. They would not fight or denigrate white people. They would simply resist by walking instead of riding, causing a financial drain on the white-owned bus companies, which had profited from the thousands of black riders while treating them like second-class citizens.

For 12 months adults and children refused to ride the buses, no matter the hardship. For 12 months Martin received daily death threats from those who opposed the boycott. But he never backed away from the mantle of leadership, not even on the night in January 1956 when the Ku Klux Klan (KKK) bombed his house while Coretta and Yolanda slept inside. (The KKK, a secret society founded after the Civil War, used threats and violence to oppress black people.) He stayed up late into the night, trying to pray. How could he love those who hated him? When he asked God to remove his bitterness, an inner voice told him to stand up for justice and truth. It filled him with peace and sustained him during the many challenges in the years ahead.

In December 1956 the US Supreme Court ruled that Alabama's segregation laws were unconstitutional. Black riders in Montgomery could sit at the front of the bus or anywhere they wanted. The direct action protest had accomplished something thought impossible. The protestors had won a battle against segregation and knocked down Jim Crow.

Martin became a hero to black Americans across the country and was propelled into the leadership of a growing civil rights movement. He received letters of support and funds from black and white people all over America. Ralph Bunche, the 1950 Nobel Peace Prize winner, sent him a telegram, lauding his quiet courage. *Time* magazine featured 28-year-old Martin on the cover.

But Martin and Ralph struggled with the next step. They wanted to build on the momentum of the bus boycott and launch another protest. But where, and for what? How could they protest places where they weren't even allowed inside, like restaurants and movie theaters?

During the boycott Martin and Ralph had become an unbeatable team. Martin provided the strategy and philosophy, while Ralph handled the logistics of communication and organization. Both ministers shared a desire to continue this fight against injustice. Martin believed that any movement for social change had to be rooted in the religious life of black people. In 1957 he and Ralph and 50 other ministers in communities around the South started the Southern Christian Leadership Conference. Martin was elected president. They began planning their next campaign, a voter registration drive.

In 1959 Martin and Coretta traveled to India to learn more about Gandhi's philosophy. After that trip Martin was convinced that nonviolent resistance was the only logical and moral approach to solving the race problem. He dreamed of a Beloved Community spreading across America, battling injustice, not people, and choosing love over hate.

———— ★ ————

After law school, Bobby Kennedy wanted to launch out on his own. He and his wife, Ethel, (born Ethel Skakel) had already started a family with the birth of their daughter Kathleen in 1951. But when asked to help rescue his brother's floundering 1952 Senate race, he could not refuse his father's request. Bobby had learned a great deal since Jack's first campaign in 1946. Because this was a statewide contest, Bobby developed a hardworking crew of young volunteers to work for Jack all over Massachusetts. His laser focus and attention to detail turned the campaign around.

Afterward Jack credited Bobby's sharp political skills for his victory. "I don't know what Bobby does," he told a reporter, "but it always seems to turn out right."

The two brothers were now a team.

Following the campaign, Bobby served a short time on the Senate Permanent Subcommittee on Investigations during the reign of Republican senator Joe McCarthy. The hunt to rid the federal government of suspected Communists was at a fever pitch, and innocent people were charged without cause. Bobby deeply feared the spread of Communism, but after six months he questioned the committee's tactics and resigned.

Later he took a position as chief legal counsel for the Senate Rackets Committee, which was investigating criminal behavior in the trade union movement. The hearings were televised nationwide. Bobby took on the powerful union leader Jimmy Hoffa, accusing him of corruption and refusing to be cowed. His performance earned him a reputation for arrogance, ruthlessness, and determination. At

Bobby, chief counsel for the Senate Rackets Committee, listens with committee member Senator Jack Kennedy during a hearing in 1959.

this time in his life, Bobby divided the world into black and white, good guys and bad guys. Hoffa was a bad guy.

Ethel brought the children to Capitol Hill to see their father in action. Jack also served on the committee, and together the two brothers made quite an impression, appearing on magazine covers and giving interviews. The attention helped pave the way for JFK's 1960 presidential run.

Bobby loved the work, but as 1959 came to a close, he knew that he must resign and devote his full attention to building a national campaign organization for his brother. Family always came first.

During the Democratic primary campaign, JFK's religion caused problems. No Catholic had ever been elected president. Many voters feared that the Pope in Rome, head of the Catholic Church, would influence affairs in the White House. JFK won over voters by directly addressing their concerns. "Nobody asked me if I was a Catholic when I joined the United States Navy. Nobody asked my brother Joe if he was Catholic or Protestant before he climbed into an American bomber plane to fly his last mission."

JFK won the Democratic nomination, and the Kennedy brothers selected Senator Lyndon B. Johnson of Texas for the vice presidential spot on the ticket to help win over Southern voters.

By September the general election race against Republican Richard Nixon was too close to call. JFK needed the support of both black and white voters to win. "We're in trouble with Negroes," Bobby admitted. "We don't know much about civil rights." Black entertainer and activist Harry Belafonte advised Bobby that the support of Martin Luther King Jr. was the key to winning over black voters. Martin was the leader, the most recognized face of the national civil rights movement. Yet it seemed that Bobby knew little about him.

Martin and Jack Kennedy had met briefly in June. But afterward Martin told Belafonte that the candidate's concern about racism seemed more intellectual than personal. "He [Kennedy] had never had the personal experience of knowing the deep groans and passionate yearnings of the Negro for freedom," Martin said.

The Kennedys believed the prejudice they had experienced as Irish Catholics gave them insight into racism. In some ways it did. But like millions of white Americans, Jack and Bobby had never experienced how demeaning and dehumanizing it was to sit in the back of the bus or get attacked by police just for the color of their skin. JFK walked a fine line. Democratic Party members in the South supported the separation of the races; JFK did not. But he needed Southern Democrats' support and didn't want to lose their votes by getting too friendly with black leaders.

Two weeks before the election, Martin had other things on his mind. Since February, 50,000 college students across the South had protested in sit-ins to end segregation at restaurants, public swimming pools, and movie theaters. The Student Nonviolent Coordinating Committee (SNCC) organized the protests. Even though direct action protest was the SCLC's mission too, for months the group's members had stayed on the sidelines.

Martin and Coretta had moved their family to Atlanta in January 1960. Martin became assistant pastor at Ebenezer Baptist Church, where he had thrived as a child growing up. This move allowed Martin to work with his father and have more time to give speeches around the country and raise funds for the SCLC. Martin had been too busy to participate in local protests. But in October, when Atlanta college students challenged Martin to join their sit-in, he knew that he must join in. Daddy King urged him to wait until after the election. But Martin worried that the SCLC would be left behind in civil rights activism if it didn't publicly support the sit-ins.

On October 19, Martin and his brother, A.D., sat in the white-only section at the lunch counter in Rich's Department Store. That afternoon they were arrested along with 80 other protestors around the city. The pressure soon worked. The next morning Atlanta business leaders dropped the charges against the protestors and agreed to integrate downtown restaurants. Martin's brother and the students were released. But Martin was transferred to nearby DeKalb County because his arrest violated the probation for his May 1960 traffic ticket for driving without a current Georgia license. The judge sentenced him to six months of hard labor. This meant working on a chain gang with white prisoners, many of whom would have liked nothing better than to lynch him, to hang him in a tree in the dark of night.

SCLC board members sent telegrams to both presidential candidates, requesting help to get their leader out of jail. Neither Kennedy nor Nixon wanted to alienate Southern white voters, so both campaigns delayed taking action. Coretta, fearful that her husband would soon be killed, contacted her friend Harris Wofford, a Kennedy adviser.

Wofford convinced others in the civil rights division of the campaign that they needed to persuade the senator to show his concern. JFK agreed to make a call to Mrs. King.

Bobby was livid when he heard about the phone call and chewed out the team. "Do you know that three Southern governors have told us that if Jack supported Martin Luther King . . . they would throw their states to Nixon? Do you know that this election may be razor close and you have probably lost it for us?"

But four hours later Bobby had cooled off. A white driver would never have been given such a harsh penalty for a menial offense. He called the judge, informing him that it was not a political phone call, but a call from a lawyer who believed in the right of a defendant to be out on bail before his trial. "If you are a decent American you will let King out by sundown."

The next morning Judge Mitchell released Martin on $2,000 bail, noting pressure from both campaigns, though in fact he had not heard from Richard Nixon. Afterward Martin met with reporters. "I am deeply indebted to Senator Kennedy, who served as a great force in making my release possible. He exhibited moral courage of the highest order. . . . There are moments when the politically expedient can be morally wise."

Martin knew that the Kennedys wanted it both ways: to help him but also to keep the support of Southern white voters. This time they pulled it off because black newspapers covered Martin's prison story in depth, while white newspapers barely mentioned it.

Martin receives a welcome-home kiss from his wife, Coretta, upon his release from Reidsville State Prison. Their children, Yolanda, age five, and Martin Luther III, age three, and Martin's sister, Christine, join in the celebration.

On November 8, John F. Kennedy won one of the closest presidential elections in history. The support of 68
percent of black voters made all the difference. Martin
became known as the "Negro whose name determined a
president." And civil rights activists believed they finally
had a president in the White House who would support
equal rights.

Joe Sr. urged Jack to name Bobby to a cabinet position,
insisting that his son needed someone loyal and trustwor-
thy by his side. Many politicians counseled otherwise. It
was nepotism, favoritism toward family, to appoint a rel-
ative, and JFK's younger, inexperienced brother was not
qualified to be attorney general. Bobby himself was reluctant to take the position. The attorney general would handle any racial upheaval and the Southern white resistance
looming on the horizon. This position should be JFK's least
controversial appointment, and naming his brother would
just bring more attention, rather than less.

But JFK followed his father's advice and convinced
Bobby to sign on.

As head of the Justice Department, it would be Bobby's
job to address civil rights matters in the new administration—and Martin's job as head of the SCLC to make sure
that Bobby did it fairly and thoroughly.

7

"THE TIME HAS COME FOR THIS NATION TO FULFILL ITS PROMISE"

"Let the word go forth . . . that the torch has been passed to a new generation. . . . Ask not what your country can do for you—ask what you can do for your country." President John F. Kennedy's words on his inauguration day, January 20, 1961, set the tone for the country and especially inspired young Americans.

On May 4, 1961, 13 Freedom Riders (7 black, 6 white) believed they were following their president's mandate by calling attention to the inequality of segregation. Traveling on Greyhound and Trailways buses from Washington, DC, to New Orleans, they planned to challenge the separate seating and segregated bus depots in cities throughout the South through nonviolent resistance.

For the first ten days the Freedom Riders faced little resistance. But when they arrived in Anniston, Alabama,

Since the Civil War, signs like this one at a Durham, North Carolina, bus station segregated people of color into separate and inferior public facilities.

on May 14, Ku Klux Klan members dragged them off the bus and beat them with baseball bats, bottles, and lead pipes. In spite of their injuries, the riders traveled on to Birmingham, where the attacks continued.

Photos of the brutal attacks filled the front pages of newspapers around the country. Americans in the North, especially the Kennedys, were shocked by the racial hatred. The attorney general was disturbed by the violence but didn't understand why the riders would risk their lives. The president instructed Bobby to stop the protest. Bobby said he could encourage the riders to end the protest but reminded his brother that the Constitution protected their right to free speech. The federal court had also ruled in December 1960 that segregated seating in interstate travel was unconstitutional.

Martin contacted Bobby, demanding that the Department of Justice protect the riders. Martin and the SCLC hadn't started the Freedom Rides, but as the best-known civil rights spokesperson, he often advocated with government officials for the safety of protestors against segregation. Bobby told Martin that it was the federal government's job to make sure the riders were not physically attacked. But since military soldiers and federal marshals could not patrol the roads and bus stations permanently, he would use the full power of the Department of Justice to convince state authorities and local police to do their jobs.

Yet when the riders continued to Montgomery, Alabama, they were attacked again by another frenzied mob with no police in sight. Local black residents helped the riders escape from the station and offered them sanctuary in their homes. The next night 1,500 supporters of the Freedom Riders, many of them veterans of the 1954 bus boycott, gathered for a rally at Ralph Abernathy's First Baptist Church in downtown Montgomery. Outside, 3,000 segregationists had surrounded the church, setting off firebombs as federal marshals sent by Bobby Kennedy struggled to control the agitated gathering.

When the mob began throwing rocks through the church windows, Martin rushed to the basement and called Bobby. Innocent people were going to be hurt, even killed, if the attorney general didn't send in military troops to protect them. The federal marshals did not have the training to stop the violence. But Martin could not convince Bobby to take this step.

During three more phone calls that night Bobby kept reassuring Martin that additional marshals were on their way. But the crowd outside grew more violent. When Bobby heard people singing church hymns in the background, he joked, "As long as you're in church, Reverend King, and our men are down there, you might as well say a prayer for us."

Martin did not laugh. The people in the church needed prayers and the attorney general's protection. When the mob reached the church door, Martin warned Bobby that a bloody confrontation would soon take place.

All through the night Bobby had been trying to reach Alabama governor John Patterson to request that he send in the Alabama National Guard soldiers, but Patterson refused to take Bobby's calls. Patterson had supported JFK in 1960 and didn't understand why a Kennedy was putting him in a difficult political position with his segregationist supporters.

When Patterson never contacted him, Bobby finally did what Martin requested. He asked the president to sign an executive order sending troops to Montgomery. When Governor Patterson heard the news, he called Bobby immediately. He told the attorney general how upset he was that his supporters would think he had caved in to black people.

But Patterson had no choice. The president had spoken. At 4:00 AM the governor ordered 800 Alabama National Guardsmen to break up the crowd and escort the church-goers home in armored trucks.

That night Bobby finally protected the riders. He knew it was the right and moral thing to do. But when the rides continued into Mississippi and supporters poured in from all over the country, he was frustrated to be put in a difficult political situation yet again. The publicity made the president look bad, just as he was about to participate in a summit with other world leaders. Bobby called Martin, asking him to use his influence to end the protest.

Martin responded that he could not do that. "You must understand that we've made no gains without pressure and I hope that pressure will always be moral, legal and peaceful."

Earlier Martin had suggested that the Interstate Commerce Commission (ICC) could adopt regulations prohibiting segregation on interstate travel. Initially Bobby had ignored the idea, but on May 29 he petitioned the ICC to do exactly that. On September 22 the ICC issued new regulations. The WHITE and COLORED ONLY signs in interstate bus terminals around the South came down. The courageous Freedom Riders had demonstrated that ordinary citizens could change public policy through nonviolent resistance.

Martin warned the Kennedys that protests like the Freedom Rides would escalate until legislation ending segregation in public places passed in Congress. President Kennedy told Martin they didn't have enough votes because no Southern legislator would support such a bill. Bobby didn't think Martin understood the difficult political process of getting a bill passed in Congress.

Martin didn't understand Bobby's inability to grasp the deep pain and injustice of racism. But he patiently endured the slow way in which Bobby learned from experience; Martin recognized Bobby's potential sooner than most civil rights activists did. "Somewhere in this man sits good," he told his lieutenants. "Our task is to find his moral center and win him to our cause."

By late 1962 Martin felt the pressure of leading 19 million black people. He wasn't an elected official, but he was invited to give speeches all over the country, and he felt personally responsible to bring civil rights concerns to light and lead more successful protests. There had been many protests against segregation in the past two years, but few gains had been made since the Freedom Rides. It was almost impossible to battle segregation laws that had been entrenched in the South for almost 100 years, supported by a 250-year history of enslaving black Americans.

Some civil rights leaders wondered if Martin was just another preacher who could talk well. Martin knew that the movement needed another victory to arouse the conscience of the nation and the president.

Early in 1963 Martin and his SCLC lieutenants decided to launch a massive protest in Birmingham, Alabama, one of the most racially divided cities in the United States.

Birmingham had no black police officers, firefighters, sales clerks, bus drivers, or bank tellers. The unemployment rate for black people was two and a half times higher than for whites, and their average income less than half. Fifty unsolved bombings of black homes and churches had earned the city the nickname "Bombingham." But the SCLC determined that if segregation could be stopped in the most racist city in America, it could end anywhere.

Project C (Confrontation) comprised a series of sit-ins and marches to provoke mass arrests by local police, filling the jails with protesters to attract media attention and force the city government to negotiate. The protests began in late March. But three weeks later, police attacks against the protestors and employers threatening them with job loss caused many protestors to drop out. Martin debated with his lieutenants and father about what to do and then prayed about his next step.

When Birmingham's commissioner of public safety Eugene "Bull" Connor obtained an injunction from the court to prevent public protests altogether, Martin knew drastic action was needed. On Good Friday, April 12, Martin and Ralph led a march anyway; they were arrested and put in solitary confinement. When Coretta didn't receive a phone call after two days, she called Bobby and asked for help. He contacted the local officials, and on Easter Sunday evening Coretta received a phone call from her husband. Martin's lawyer was allowed to visit him in jail. He brought Martin a copy of the *Birmingham Herald* in which a published letter written by a rabbi, a Catholic priest, and six Protestant ministers criticized the two men for their "ungodly actions."

Martin was angry and perplexed. Nonviolent protest was modeled after the moral teachings of Jesus himself. How could these ministers consider themselves Christian and support a city government that allowed the bombing of black houses and churches?

From his jail cell, Martin wrote a 7,000-word passionate defense of the civil rights movement and direct action protest, filled with scriptural and historical references. He told the ministers that black people had waited 340 years for their constitutional and God-given rights, ever since they'd been kidnapped and brought to America as slaves. The time for waiting was over. "Injustice anywhere is a threat to justice everywhere," he wrote.

That's why they were protesting in Birmingham. Everyone was affected by injustice, no matter where it took place, and everyone had a responsibility to end it.

Martin wasn't just addressing the white ministers. He was speaking to black ministers who wouldn't participate in protests, the Kennedys, white Southerners, and all Americans who didn't support an end to racial segregation.

When Martin and Ralph were released several days later, participation in the protests had dropped even lower. The movement had no more money to post bail for the protestors who had been sitting in jail for weeks. Jim Bevel offered a solution. He and fellow civil rights activist Diane Nash had been training local teens in nonviolent protest methods, and the young people were determined to march.

Martin did not want to put young people in such danger, but he knew it might be their last chance to turn things around. Surely no policemen, no matter how racist, would attack children and teens. He gave his approval.

On May 2, wave after wave of young protestors departed the 16th Street Baptist Church, headed for downtown Birmingham. The Birmingham Children's Campaign had begun. When police pointed their guns and ordered the marchers to return to the church, the young people dropped

A 17-year-old marcher being attacked by a police dog. The photo appeared on the front page of the *New York Times* and led to President Kennedy's comments to reporters.

to their knees instead. Hundreds of children and teenagers were arrested that day, filling the jail to overflowing. The next morning, when new marchers took to the streets, Bull Connor ordered his men to release police dogs and use fire hoses. The dogs attacked the children's clothing, biting their legs, arms, and even their stomachs, and fire hoses with powerful water pressure knocked the marchers to the ground or up against buildings.

Cameras captured the scene, and Americans were horrified as they watched the violence unfold on their TV screens.

The White House was watching too. When Bobby stared at the television and heard the screams of the young people, something shifted inside him. "What if this were our children?" he asked his brother.

President Kennedy told reporters that the attacks made him "sick." He called Martin and demanded the protest be stopped. "The children have been suffering for two hundred years, Mr. President," Martin replied.

Support for the children of Birmingham spread throughout the country. Bobby was devastated by the violence and admitted to family friend and adviser Arthur Schlesinger that the administration's efforts in civil rights had not worked. For too long they had depended on the goodwill of Southern governors and failed to realize that these leaders and local law enforcement would maintain segregation until federal law forced them to stop.

While protesting in Greensboro, North Carolina, Jesse Jackson heard Bobby Kennedy say on the radio that segregation in Birmingham was not only illegal but immoral. "He was attorney general and he said it was *immoral*, it was *wrong*. I had never heard a white man go that far before."

Finally, Bobby had uncovered his moral core, the one Martin had long believed he possessed.

Public outcry over the violence offered the president a window of opportunity to propose civil rights legislation, he told his brother. But JFK and his other advisers still worried that such a controversial bill would tie up Congress for a year and could cost him the 1964 election.

Bobby kept trying to persuade his brother. As president, JFK could no longer speak abroad about American democracy when black citizens at home faced inequality and violence. He could sell the bill by speaking to the heart of the problem: segregation was morally wrong.

But JFK was still not convinced—until June 11. That morning he read Martin's challenging words on the front page of the *New York Times*: "President Kennedy must begin talking about race as a moral issue, in terms never heard from the White House before."

That afternoon the president watched on national television as Governor George Wallace blocked a doorway at the University of Alabama, defying Kennedy's executive order to allow two black students to enroll.

Enough was enough.

That evening President Kennedy spoke to the nation, explaining how segregation clashed with America's democratic and religious traditions: "The heart of the question is whether all Americans are to be afforded equal rights and equal opportunities. . . . Are we to say to the world, and much more importantly, to each other that this is a land of the free except for the Negroes, that we have no second-class citizens except Negroes. . . . Now the time has come for this nation to fulfill its promise."

Noting the violence in Birmingham, and the children who had been attacked just for marching, JFK ended his speech by announcing that he would send a civil rights bill to Congress within the week.

Martin was thrilled and sent the president a telegram, commending him on his plea for justice and freedom for all Americans. But hours later the joy turned to sadness and outrage when NAACP activist Medgar Evers was murdered by a Klan member in the driveway of his Mississippi home, while his wife and children awaited him inside.

8

"I HAVE A DREAM"

President Kennedy assigned the attorney general to oversee the writing of the historic bill and its defense at congressional committee hearings. Bobby fulfilled both jobs with passion. "We have demanded that the Negro obey the same laws as white men, pay the same taxes, fight and die in the same wars," he told the House Rules Committee in July. "Yet in nearly every part of the country, he remains the victim of humiliation and deprivation no white citizen would tolerate."

That same month Bobby approached SNCC leader John Lewis at a civil rights meeting. "The young people have educated me, John," he said. "You have changed me." John was shocked that the attorney general who had been so reluctant to support them during the Freedom Rides had grown so much in recognizing that people of color deserved equal rights and in leading the Department of Justice to make changes.

On June 22, Martin, Bobby, Vice President Johnson, Roy Wilkins (executive secretary of the NAACP), and other leaders gathered in the Rose Garden following a White House conference on civil rights.

Yet Bobby never expressed such thoughts to Martin. After all the two men had been through, the phone calls, letters, and telegrams, they had met in large gatherings at the White House but never privately. Bobby believed that he could not fully trust Martin because two of Martin's closest advisers had been accused by the FBI of being members of the American Communist Party. In Bobby's mind, there could be no greater danger than a person who supported the spread of Communism.

By early August, momentum for a national civil rights event, the March on Washington, had skyrocketed. The march was planned by a joint effort of eight civil rights groups, and attendees had signed on from all 50 states. The president and attorney general were concerned about possible rioting and the political fallout for the civil rights bill if the march were to fail. But civil rights leaders refused to cancel the event. In the end, Bobby put the full weight of the Justice Department behind the march to help ensure a successful execution of the huge protest.

On August 28 black and white Americans traveled to the capital by train, bus, airplane, and automobile.

After a long day of music and speeches, Martin was finally introduced as "Martin Luther King, the moral leader of the country." He concluded the celebration with one of the most famous speeches in American history, poetically encapsulating the civil rights movement's yearning for equality. His words mesmerized the 250,000 marchers and the millions who watched on television at home.

"I have a dream . . . that my four little children will one day live in a nation where they will not be judged by the color of their skin but by the content of their character."

The Kennedys watched from the White House. "One of the best speeches I have ever heard," the president said.

JFK should know. His inaugural address is considered one of the finest presidential speeches in history. After Martin spoke, civil rights leaders gathered at the White House for a reception in their honor.

On September 15 the hope and optimism generated during the March on Washington was shattered. That Sunday morning an explosion ripped through the 16th Street Baptist Church in Birmingham, the very place from which the brave children had begun marching in May. Four young girls were killed and 22 church members injured

Edith Lee arrived from Detroit, Michigan. It was her 12th birthday and she was "glad to be standing with people who wanted to make things right."

from a dynamite blast caused by a bomb planted by KKK members.

Rioting broke out in the black neighborhoods, and Martin rushed back to Birmingham to persuade people that violence would neither end their pain nor bring progress. But he understood their grief and offered no solutions the following week when he met with President Kennedy and the attorney general.

———— ★ ————

Bobby had begun to question FBI director J. Edgar Hoover's obsession with Martin and his possible connection with the Communist Party. But after months of pressure from Hoover, on October 10 Bobby finally approved the wiretapping of Martin's telephones. The FBI would connect a listening device to his telephone in order to secretly monitor his conversations. Any hint that Martin had associated with Communists could damage the civil rights bill and the president's reelection chances. The Kennedys could not take that chance.

No evidence was ever found that Martin was involved with the Communist Party. Bobby later regretted authorizing the FBI wiretaps but did not stop the order before he resigned as attorney general in 1964, and it remained in place until 1966. For the unwarranted and unconstitutional monitoring of their leader, some activists distrusted Bobby for the rest of his public life. But many black voters were devoted to him and supportive during his presidential run in 1968, including Martin. MLK biographer David Garrow believes that if not for these accusations about a Communist connection, "the Kennedy and Johnson Administrations would most likely have embraced both King and the entire southern black freedom struggle far more warmly than they did."

Martin's phone calls did reveal his extramarital affairs. Considered a prophet by so many, he was well aware of his own human failings and never held himself above other people. Garrow believes that important insights about Martin can be learned from the recorded phone calls. "You see him being intensely self-critical. King really and truly believed that he was there to be of service to others."

On November 22 another violent event took away all vestiges of the summer's optimism about civil rights. President Kennedy was shot in Dallas, Texas, while riding in a motorcade with his wife, Jackie. When the news hit the airwaves, Americans rushed to church to pray or huddled around portable radios and television sets, waiting for updates about their president's condition.

One hour later Walter Cronkite of CBS News confirmed the news the country dreaded hearing: "President Kennedy died at 1 PM Central Standard Time, 2:00 Eastern Standard Time." The newscaster's voice never broke, but as he formed the words Cronkite took off his glasses to gather his emotions.

When Martin heard the news that the president had been killed, he grabbed his wife's hand. "Corrie, this is what is going to happen to me also," he told her.

Martin was deeply disturbed by the assassination. In spite of their struggles, he felt a kinship with the president, grateful for his cautious yet growing support for civil rights.

Bobby was holding a meeting at his home when FBI Director Hoover called with the news that the president had been shot. Bobby numbly went into action, handing out assignments to aides and to family members who began to arrive.

When his brother's death was confirmed 30 minutes later, his children had just returned from school. Holding them close, he said, "Uncle Jack had the most wonderful life."

Then he flew by helicopter to Andrews Air Force Base, where he hid from reporters in the back of a truck. Tears streamed down his face as he waited for Jackie, his brother's body, and the new president—Lyndon B. Johnson.

Americans were deeply saddened and troubled by the shocking loss. The assassination of their vibrant president marked the start of a darker era for many Americans. If their president, the leader of the free world, could be killed, maybe the United States wasn't the strongest nation in the world after all. Who hated America that much? they wondered. Were the Russians trying to take over the country?

For four days Americans stayed glued to their television sets, watching as mourners walked by the president's casket in the Capitol Rotunda, as JFK's son John-John saluted his father's coffin, and daughter Caroline grasped her mother's hand and held her doll close to her heart. Thousands lined the street to watch the procession down Pennsylvania Avenue. Bobby and younger brother Ted walked on either side of Jackie, behind six horses pulling a flag-draped casket and soldiers playing muffled drums.

The night of the funeral, President Johnson called Martin and promised to back the civil rights bill with all his might. Johnson was a Southerner from Texas, and Martin was relieved to hear of his support.

Johnson asked Bobby to stay on as attorney general and continue to spearhead the civil rights bill's passage through Congress. Deeply grieving, Bobby agreed, though he knew it would be difficult. This legislation would define his brother's legacy on civil rights and help black Americans more than any federal action ever had.

Now the oldest Kennedy son, Bobby kept the clan together with love and the steely drive his father always said he possessed. But he struggled with the loss of his brother and best friend. For the past 12 years, JFK's political career had been Bobby's entire professional focus. "It was as though he had lost both his arms," Ethel said.

For consolation, he turned to his Catholic faith, the writings of the French philosopher Albert Camus on the meaning of death, and ancient Greek writings on the role of suffering in human lives. Jackie had lent him Edith Hamilton's book *The Greek Way*, and Bobby found comfort in memorizing lines from the book, such as these from Aeschylus's play *Agamemnon*: "He who learns must suffer. And even in our sleep, pain which cannot forget falls drop by drop upon the heart, and in our own despair, against our will, comes wisdom to us by the awful grace of God."

Ideas like this helped him learn to trust that through God's grace he would somehow survive his deep suffering and grief. Facing his own pain helped him be more patient and tolerant, more compassionate toward others and their suffering.

In spite of LBJ's support, by year's end, the civil rights bill still languished in the House Rules Committee. But over the December holiday break, citizens who'd witnessed the violence against the children of Birmingham and the joy of the March on Washington pressured their congressional representatives to support the legislation.

After weeks of public hearings, lobbying by thousands of activists and civil rights leaders, letters from churchgoers to their representatives, pressure from both Democratic and Republican voters, and the bipartisan support of both Republicans and Democrats in Congress, the House passed the bill in February. Then it was the Senate's turn. Southerners in the Senate finally succumbed to the pressure in June to allow the Senate to follow suit. The law would be official when LBJ signed the legislation.

Martin was overjoyed. July 2, 1964, should have been a happy day for Bobby too. But this was his brother's legislation. Jack should have been behind the desk signing the bill, not Johnson. Bobby hung back until his assistants called him forward, and the president finally acknowledged his presence and gave him one of the signing pens as a souvenir of the occasion.

Martin was struck by the sadness in Bobby's eyes. He wrote him a letter afterward, thanking him for his passionate support of the bill.

The celebration was also muted by the recent murders of three civil rights workers in Mississippi, killed by the KKK for setting up Freedom Schools and registering black voters.

At the Democratic convention in late August, Bobby gave a moving tribute to his brother in his introduction of a film about JFK's life and legacy. Delegates in the convention hall stood and applauded for 22 minutes before they let him speak.

On September 3, Bobby resigned as attorney general. He had considered leaving public life and going into teaching. He'd asked President Johnson to appoint him ambassador to South Vietnam because he believed he could help address America's complex involvement in Vietnam. Johnson never responded to Bobby's request.

In the end Bobby decided that he could best serve the country by staying in politics. He ran for the US Senate seat from New York State and won a close race over the Republican incumbent with help from the overwhelming victory of Johnson and his new vice president, Hubert Humphrey. For the last four years, Bobby had spoken almost solely on behalf of his brother. Now, as a newly elected senator, he had to decide what he—Bobby Kennedy—truly stood for.

9

"A TINY RIPPLE OF HOPE"

In the summer of 1964, Lyndon Johnson launched a War on Poverty with numerous programs addressing unemployment, housing, and health issues for the poor. Bobby supported these important initiatives and served on the Senate committee reviewing their effectiveness. But he also began searching for other ways to help solve the nation's poverty problems, visiting low-income neighborhoods, American Indian reservations, and the farmworkers on strike in California. He explored how businesses could help through public-private initiatives, such as the one in Brooklyn, New York. There, local businesses provided jobs in addition to government programs to help people in the Bedford-Stuyvesant neighborhood.

Martin was always on the road, giving speeches, raising funds for the SCLC, and supporting the next demonstration for equal rights. He had little time to relax or joke around with friends and family. But he tried to return

Bobby loved to visit with children wherever he traveled. This photo shows him meeting children in Brooklyn's Bedford-Stuyvesant neighborhood in February 1966.

home every Sunday to preach at Ebenezer Baptist Church. He spent the day with his family, eating Sunday dinner and playing with his children in the backyard. Years later Yolanda, Martin's oldest child, said, "He was our partner in crime. My memories are full of laughter. I just remember laughing, laughing."

One Sunday he received word that he'd won the Nobel Peace Prize for his leadership in promoting nonviolent resistance to end racial segregation in America. The youngest person ever to receive the international award, Martin was humbled by the honor and used his new platform to support freedom movements around the world. After the award ceremony in December 1964, he was offered many opportunities, including professorships at prestigious universities. But he would not leave the movement he cherished. He kept working on his deep belief that America could become a Beloved Community in which the rights of all people are respected.

The Civil Rights Act was now on the books, and legal segregation had ended. But many black Southerners could not vote. They had to pass a complex literacy test just to register. In the spring of 1965, Martin, the SCLC, and members of the SNCC launched a voting campaign in Selma, Alabama. After weeks of local marches and attempts to register black voters at the county courthouse proved fruitless, leaders decided on a massive 31-mile march from Selma to the statehouse in Montgomery to call on Governor George Wallace. On March 7, John Lewis and Hosea Williams led 800 marchers onto Edmund Pettus Bridge and were brutally attacked by state police.

Martin sent out a national call to religious leaders and supporters to join their efforts. Overnight, thousands poured into the city, turning the local protest into a national movement. But only after Boston minister James Reeb was beaten and killed one night by white supremacists did President Johnson finally call on Congress to enact a strong voting rights bill.

The president ended his speech before Congress with the words "We shall overcome," the rallying cry of the civil rights movement. As they listened in Selma, John Lewis watched as tears rolled down Martin's face.

By August, Congress had passed the Voting Rights Act and LBJ had signed it into law. Bobby and his brother Ted, now a senator from Massachusetts, had lobbied for the bill on the Senate floor. Bobby had believed in the importance of protecting voting rights since his early days as attorney general.

But once again violence marred a jubilant time in the civil rights movement. Just days after the bill signing, two white policemen in the neighborhood of Watts, in Los Angeles, scuffled with a black motorist suspected of drunken driving. A crowd watched the arrest and grew angry by what they believed to be another incident of racially motivated abuse by the police.

Onlookers erupted in anger, throwing stones and bottles at the police and looting and burning down 200 local businesses. When officers attacked the rioters, the violence escalated.

After five days of rioting, 34 people were dead and 1,000 injured, most at the hands of local police or the California National Guard. Hundreds were arrested. It was the most damaging race riot in American history. Los Angeles public officials and local white residents were shocked by the violence and didn't understand the causes for the rioters' anger. Black people were frustrated about the rundown housing and overcrowded schools in their neighborhoods and racist police officers who mistreated people of color.

Martin flew to L.A. and was dismayed when he toured the decimated neighborhood. But he understood that rioting was rooted in a deep despair over poverty. When asked for the causes of the riots, he repeatedly said, "We've got to see that a riot is the language of the unheard. . . . I worked to get these people the right to eat hamburgers, and now I've got to do something . . . to help them get the money to buy them."

Several federal poverty programs had been established in Watts. But as Johnson elevated troop levels in Vietnam and war costs escalated, funding for the War on Poverty decreased before it could make a difference. Forty-three percent of black families still earned less than $2,000 ($16,000 today) a year, compared to 16 percent of white families. Martin tried to explain to the press and government officials that with no resources, black people had little stake in society and this often led to angry, dangerous behavior. In his speeches Martin began talking about how unjust it was that a small percentage of the population controlled all the wealth. He said that if economic power were redistributed, the rioting would stop.

For years Bobby had been worried about conditions in cities outside the South. In his last act as attorney general, he had sent President Johnson a memorandum entitled

"Racial Violence in Urban Centers." It discussed how the national government must help to solve problems "that have created Negro frustrations and hatreds."

A year after the Watts riots, Bobby felt even more strongly about the issue. Legal segregation had been eliminated in the South. But "Northern problems are the problems of everyday living in jobs and housing and education," he said in a speech in New York.

"He's right, Andy," Martin said to Andrew Young. "We have neglected the cities of the North."

Andrew thought the SCLC had done a great deal with its limited budget and resources. "But Martin took it seriously. He never thought he had done enough and Bobby Kennedy's words ate at him."

The SCLC had already decided to address racial problems in Northern cities like Chicago, where the hostility toward black residents could be as bad as in the Southern states. Blacks who moved north in search of better jobs usually lived in all-black neighborhoods where their children attended segregated schools. This wasn't because of segregation laws like in the South, but because low wages forced them to live in poorer neighborhoods.

———— ★ ————

Along with investigating the needs of diverse communities in America, Bobby also visited cities around the world where uprisings for freedom were taking place. In June 1966 a student group invited him to speak in South Africa at the height of apartheid, the governmental system there that had racially segregated blacks from whites since 1948. Few world leaders had dared to entangle themselves in the politics of South Africa. Martin had spoken out and had been invited to speak. But the white supremacist government in South Africa had refused to issue him a travel visa. But being a Kennedy and a likely US president someday, Bobby had no trouble getting a visa from South African officials.

During the visit he and Ethel met with the apartheid protestors, and Bobby shared America's long history of racial struggles and its current progress. At the University of Cape Town, he gave his famous Day of Affirmation speech that is often quoted by activists today.

Back home, voices against the Vietnam War had grown louder. Both Bobby and Martin privately questioned

> "*Each time a man stands up for an ideal, or acts to improve the lot of others, or strikes out against injustice, he sends forth a tiny ripple of hope, and crossing each other from a million different centers of energy and daring those ripples build a current which can sweep down the mightiest walls of oppression and resistance.*"
> —Senator Robert F. Kennedy

America's growing involvement in the war while citizens were dying of poverty and violence at home. Bobby spoke with Johnson several times about his concerns but was torn about his own position. During his brother's presidency, JFK had sent military advisers to Vietnam and supported a corrupt South Vietnamese government in hopes of preventing the Communists in North Vietnam from gaining a stronghold. Should Bobby continue to protect the legacy of his brother's involvement or publicly articulate his doubts about the war? What would Jack have decided now about Vietnam, if he were still alive?

Since the early 1960s, Martin had shared his concerns about Vietnam with close friends. Although black Americans bore some of the heaviest burdens in the war, they were still denied basic freedoms at home. Vietnam marked the first major combat deployment of an integrated military, and the first time African American enlistment was encouraged. Yet black soldiers signed up not because they finally could but because they had no other option; many had no job to earn a decent living. Most of the black recruits were assigned to the infantry, serving on the front line, so they were the first to die in battle. Despite accounting for 11 percent of the total troops in Vietnam, they represented only 2 percent of the officer corps. But Martin didn't speak out publicly; he feared affecting President Johnson's support of civil rights issues.

By early 1967, 500,000 American troops fought in Vietnam, and President Johnson had shown no willingness to enter peace talks or stop the bombing of North Vietnam.

Americans were divided about the war. Like Bobby and Martin, most political figures hesitated to take on a president determined to win the war at any cost.

Bobby began to challenge the whole basis of the war, questioning his long-held belief in the domino theory—that if South Vietnam fell to the Communists, the neighboring countries of Cambodia and Laos would too, putting the security of America at risk. In February 1967, Bobby met with Johnson and pleaded with him to negotiate a cease-fire with North Vietnam. The president promised to do so but took no action.

Antiwar activists begged Bobby to challenge Johnson for the presidency in the 1968 election. He decided that he would not challenge a standing president of his own party, but he could no longer remain silent about the war. On March 2 he stood on the Senate floor and apologized for being part of a Kennedy administration that had first sent advisory troops to Vietnam. He talked about a war fought mostly by young men of color and outlined a three-point plan to end the conflict, including a suspension of bombing in North Vietnam and eventual withdrawal of all American soldiers. Johnson was furious, and the next week he increased troop levels.

A month later Martin told a huge crowd at Riverside Church in New York City that the war was wrong and that violence in Vietnam and on the streets in America must end. "A nation that continues year after year to spend more money on military defense than on programs of social uplift is approaching spiritual death," he said.

After years of silence, Martin was relieved to finally speak publicly against the war. But criticism came from all fronts—SCLC advisers, the NAACP, the press, even black newspapers and many of his followers. Stick to equality at home, they said. Peace and civil rights don't mix. Johnson felt betrayed and never invited Martin to the White House again. But Martin didn't let that stop him from participating in war protests all over the country.

In April Bobby traveled to Mississippi with other congressional representatives and was dismayed by the widespread poverty he witnessed. Afterward he met with Marian Wright, the Mississippi lawyer who had arranged the trip. "The only way there's going to be change is if it's more uncomfortable for Congress not to act than it is for them to act. . . . You've got to get a whole lot of poor people who just come to Washington and stay here until Congress gets really embarrassed and they have to act," he told her.

Wright told Bobby that Dr. King already had a similar plan. So Bobby wrote Martin a letter, encouraging the new campaign and offering his support. Martin believed that all races must work together to find solutions to poverty and turn poor people power into a political movement. SCLC board members began contacting representatives of American Indian tribes, Hispanics, poor whites, and young black gang members, inviting them to join a new protest called the Poor People's Campaign. Coretta watched her husband's spirits lift. For years people had looked to him for solutions to end poverty, and now he finally had a plan.

Just as Martin had long predicted, the riots continued. Little federal help had been offered to low-income urban areas since the riot in Watts two years earlier. During the summer of 1967, racial unrest escalated, often ignited by violent encounters with police. To many white Americans, it seemed as if the country were splitting in two. In desperation, President Johnson appointed the President's National Advisory Commission on Civil Disorders—known as the Kerner Commission—to investigate the causes of the race riots. Bobby and Martin knew the causes and could have advised the president. But because of their public criticism of the Vietnam War, neither was consulted.

After Bobby's public statements against the war, he did not speak or meet with President Johnson for over a year. In a September 1967 interview he said, "Now I know how Negroes who riot feel. I have no influence in the government that makes decisions that affect my life."

While his brother was president, Bobby had sat at the seat of power. Now he finally understood what Martin had been talking about all these years.

10

"DO THEY KNOW ABOUT MARTIN LUTHER KING?"

April 4, 1968, 8:30 PM (EST)
Indianapolis

Martin Luther King Jr. had been murdered in Memphis. But the 2,000 people at 17th and Broadway did not yet know and were awaiting the arrival of Bobby Kennedy. When organizers at the rally site heard the news over a radiophone, they rushed inside the Broadway Christian Center to discuss the situation. Snooky Hendricks reported that a militant group called the Ten Percenters had gathered near the fence and were carrying weapons. Since the police were not coming, he calmly suggested that he and Ben Bell recruit College Club members to monitor the crowd and check the trees and nearby buildings for people with guns.

John Lewis would not let himself think about Dr. King—not now, not yet. They had to protect the people at the rally and make sure that violence didn't break out.

They would be distraught that their leader, who had fought 13 years for justice for all Americans, was gone.

"You can't have a crowd like this come, and something like this happen, and send them home without anything at all," John said. "Senator Kennedy has to speak, for his own sake, and the sake of these people."

They all agreed, but only if Bobby himself told the crowd about Dr. King. But was the senator still coming? Nobody knew.

On Kennedy's plane, campaign aides discussed the situation. Should the senator cancel, out of respect for Dr. King? For his own safety? Fearing violence at the rally site, many local politicians had already canceled their participation. Rioting had erupted in Memphis and other cities across the country. Indianapolis could explode next. Campaign staff in Washington, DC, called in, urging the senator to skip the rally and go directly to the hotel. The streets of DC were already ablaze with fires set by rioters.

Bobby knew that if he spoke and violence broke out, he would be blamed. But if he did not speak and a riot started, he would still be blamed. Ethel didn't try to talk her husband out of going to the rally. She knew that her husband had to go.

Bobby stood up. "There's no way I won't give that speech. I've got to make that speech. It's the most important thing I can do."

He sat alone on the plane for a few minutes and then emerged wearing JFK's black trench coat; Bobby had worn it often since his brother's death. He made a brief statement to the press but took no questions. As he walked to his car, the chief of police approached him. "I can't protect you, Senator, if you give that speech. Instructions from the mayor."

Bobby stared at the police chief. "Chief, I could sleep on the streets of your city with my family and no one would bother us."

Then he walked over to Ethel's car, opened the door, and leaned in to give her a kiss. "Keep an eye on her," he instructed one of his aides.

Ethel made the sign of the cross as her husband walked away. All she could do now was wait back at the hotel—and pray.

As his black sedan headed toward 17th and Broadway, Bobby asked his trusted adviser Fred Dutton what to say.

"You know what to say, Bob. Just speak from your heart."

Bobby nodded. Then began scribbling notes on the back of an envelope.

The weather had turned dark and cold, with gusty winds and a drizzle of rain. Many in the crowd at the rally site had been waiting for three hours or more, but they still continued to cheer and wave signs. Altha Cravey's father had grown more nervous. Twice he had tried to convince the girls to leave, but they wouldn't budge.

Billie Breaux and her husband had just arrived. They'd rushed over from Kennedy headquarters after campaign officials had announced that the senator was running late.

He would skip the reception at the headquarters and head straight to the rally. They did not announce that Dr. King was dead.

Billie loved Bobby Kennedy. She had to see him. He was so authentic, so real. He really believed in black people and wanted to help. No other politicians had wanted to help black Americans before President Kennedy. President Eisenhower hadn't done anything. The Kennedys had seemed like the first real possibility.

John Lewis walked through the crowd. A few people on the perimeter huddled around transistor radios. But if they heard the tragic news, they didn't share it. He did not see the Ten Percenters. No one else seemed to know that Dr. King was dead.

Nineteen-year-old Darlene Howard knew. Her mother had called with the horrifying news and urged her to come over to her place. But when Darlene left her apartment, she couldn't get to her car. A huge gathering of people packed the street. The smell of gasoline filled the air and young men were waving around guns and knives. *They're going to burn down the city*, she thought.

Darlene tried to get back to the sidewalk but was trapped on all sides as the throng carried her down the street.

"He's on his way," a campaign worker reported, handing John Lewis the radiophone.

"I'm sorry, John." Senator Kennedy's voice sounded crackly and strange on the two-way radio. "You lost a leader. We all lost a leader."

John appreciated Bobby's words.

When he hung up, the crowd was still laughing and cheering, but a few militant voices now filled the air. "King didn't deserve that."

"What are you doing here, Whitey?"

"Dr. King is dead and a white man did it. Why does Kennedy have to come here?"

But others in the crowd did not react. They didn't seem to hear them.

Mary Evans heard the rumor going through the crowd. People said King had been shot, but that he was going to be OK.

John understood their anger. But they'd already lost so much this night. They could not afford any more violence.

———— ★ ————

A few blocks from the rally site, as Bobby's car approached the invisible line between white and black Indianapolis, the police escort peeled off. When he arrived, JoMarva Bell watched him get out of the car, shocked at how white his face was, "like the blood drained out of him."

When the crowd spotted the senator, those in front pushed toward him, trying to shake his hand. But this night there was no working the crowd, no Kennedy smile.

"It was like he wasn't there," a staffer said.

The cheering grew louder as Bobby headed up the steps to the platform.

People in nearby homes leaned out their windows. Teens in the trees peered over the small stage, while others perched on the side of the truck bed that served as the stage.

Bobby stood at the microphone, the wind whipping his hair. Two floodlights mounted on poles swayed in the breeze. A lone spotlight moved across the sky, leaving the crowd in shadows.

Bobby on the truck bed, as he spoke to the crowd.

Rose Cantwell watched as her husband, Paul, hovered behind the senator, his eyes flicking back and forth over the crowd. Paul had been a county commissioner and a city councilman, and now served in the state legislature. Both he and Rose worked on Bobby's local campaign, and Paul had been invited onto the truck bed with other dignitaries. Why did her husband look so nervous? Rose wondered.

Bobby turned to the men standing behind him. "Do they know about Martin Luther King?" he asked.

"We left it up to you," one of them answered.

11

"I HAVE SOME VERY SAD NEWS FOR ALL OF YOU"

"Ladies and gentlemen—I'm only going to talk to you just for a minute or so this evening. Because . . ." Bobby coughed, waiting for people to settle down. "Could you lower those signs, please?" he asked. This night he was not thinking of the race for president.

How small he looks, thought JoMarva Bell, *standing there all alone.*

"I have some very sad news for all of you, and, I think, sad news for all of our fellow citizens, and people who love peace all over the world. . . . Martin Luther King was shot and was killed tonight in Memphis, Tennessee."

Those in front were stunned into silence, while those behind continued to cheer, until Bobby's words crashed like a wave, and a huge moan reverberated through the crowd.

Loraine Minor collapsed against a tree, sobbing on her friend's shoulder. Mark Higbee felt as if he'd been punched in his stomach; he doubled over, until his father brought him gently to the ground.

"Martin Luther King . . . dedicated his life . . . to love . . . and to justice between fellow human beings. He died in the cause of that effort." Bobby's voice was so quiet, people had to lean forward to hear his words.

Martin had never stopped working for justice.

"In this difficult day, in this difficult time for the United States, it's perhaps well to ask what kind of a nation we are . . . and what direction we want to move in . . ."

Bobby's words were so similar to those he had spoken earlier in the day. But just hours later, America had changed forever.

Darlene Howard looked around. *The senator's going to be killed*, she thought.

I'm going to be killed, thought Mary Evans, as she watched young men near the fence rattling chains in their hands.

"For those of you who are black—considering the evidence evidently is that there were white people who were responsible—you can be filled with bitterness, and with hatred, and a desire for revenge . . ."

People began to murmur.

"Who killed Dr. King?" a voice cried out. "Why?"

Bobby tried to speak over the shouting. But then he stopped.

He waited a moment, gripping the envelope in his hand as he looked out. His face filled with sadness but not fear.

Jim Trulock watched his friend Ben Bell move through the crowd, reaching out, consoling the teenagers.

Altha Cravey looked at her father, certain he would now drag her and Mary out of there. But he stood quietly, waiting for Senator Kennedy to continue.

Jim Trulock (middle) campaigning with Bobby and fellow labor organizer and activist Jim Smith.

"Or we can make an effort, as Martin Luther King did, to understand and to comprehend, and replace that violence, that stain of bloodshed that has spread across our land, with an effort to understand with compassion and love."

Even when arrested or beaten by police, Martin always responded with love, determined to win them over with nonviolent resistance.

Seventeen-year-old Terri Alvies was in shock, trying to make sense of things. She stood near the front, watching the senator's caring face, his voice so peaceful and quiet, talking about Dr. King, not himself.

The crowd grew quiet again. *Like a gnat on cotton*, thought Darlene Howard.

It was as if the senator had laid his hands upon the audience and healed them, thought Mary Evans.

"For those of you who are black . . . I can only say that I feel—" His voice broke. "In my own heart the same kind of feeling. I had a member of my family killed . . ."

John Lewis was shocked. Never in the five years since President Kennedy's assassination had the senator ever talked in public about his brother's death.

Whispers carried through the crowd. Senator Kennedy understood their grief. He respected who they were. He shared their pain, thought Billie Breaux.

"My favorite poet is Aeschylus," Bobby said, and began a quote that he had memorized, a quote that had given him solace since his brother's death: "Even in our sleep, pain which cannot forget falls drop by drop upon the heart, and, in our own despair, against our will, comes wisdom through the awful grace of God."

Bobby's press secretary, Frank Mankiewicz, stood in the back of the crowd. The press bus had gotten lost on the way to the rally, and he had arrived after Bobby had begun to speak. The speech wasn't at all like he and the senator had discussed, but it felt just right.

"What we need in the United States is not division; what we need in the United States is not hatred; what we need in the United States is not violence and lawlessness, but is love and wisdom, and compassion toward one another, and a feeling of justice toward those who still suffer within our country, whether they be white or whether they be black."

The Ten Percenters put away their chains and guns. They listened as Bobby told the crowd that they needed to hold on to Martin's legacy of nonviolence and compassion, to still believe that the mistrust between white and black people could be bridged.

Jim Trulock thought it was the best speech he had ever heard.

John Lewis had heard Dr. King preach many times. Bobby's halting style was very different from Martin's oratory. Yet it was as if Bobby were channeling Martin that night.

Darlene Howard felt like he was channeling God himself.

Bobby continued, "So I ask you tonight to return home, to say a prayer for the family of Martin Luther King . . .

but more importantly to say a prayer for our own country, which all of us love."

There was no applause, no cheering as Bobby left the platform. People wept and hugged each other, even those they did not know.

Some tried to touch Bobby as he climbed down the stairs. JoMarva Bell stood close enough to call out to him. "It's the thirteenth birthday of my baby, my daughter India."

"Happy birthday," Bobby mouthed to the teenager, as he was ushered away. Bobby had 10 children. He knew how important birthdays were.

Side by side, the crowd departed, like after a funeral.

But not Darlene Howard. She ran all the way back to her apartment and locked the door. What would the crowd have done without Bobby Kennedy?

Back at home, Billie Breaux told her nine-year-old daughter Jean about Senator Kennedy's speech. "He didn't talk down to us, Jean. He spoke to us as adults, as intelligent people, and was courageous because he allowed himself to feel others' pain."

No other politician could have given that speech—not President Johnson, Hubert Humphrey, Eugene McCarthy, or Richard Nixon. Bobby Kennedy had a connection with black people. He was a wealthy white person with little experience of racial prejudice. But he knew the pain of great loss and how to put himself in someone else's shoes and feel their suffering.

12

"A TIME OF SHAME AND SORROW"

Back at the Marott Hotel, Bobby suspended all campaign activities, including his speech in Cleveland the next day—until black leaders called and urged him to come. He did not cancel a previously scheduled meeting with local black activists. At first they wanted to blame Bobby, calling him an establishment candidate who came from money.

Bobby understood that they were angry and grieving over Martin's death. But he still tried to explain his situation. "Big business is trying to defeat me because they say I am a friend of the Negro. You are down on me because you say I am part of the establishment."

After they talked with Bobby for two hours, Snooky Hendricks conceded that the senator was "completely sympathetic and understanding."

When the activists departed, Bobby threw himself down on his bed in his hotel room and cried, until he remembered that he must call Martin's wife, Coretta, and offer assistance. Over the phone she told Bobby that she needed to get her husband's body back to Atlanta. Bobby assigned John Lewis the task of chartering a plane. Then he and his staff stayed up into the early hours, writing a new speech for Cleveland.

On television, Martin's last speech the night before was broadcast over and over, followed by footage of violent uprisings across the country. By 11:00 PM riots had erupted in 30 cities, 110 by the next day. But not in Atlanta, Martin's hometown. And not in Indianapolis, where Bobby had spoken.

In Memphis, the Reverend Jim Lawson, who had urged Martin to support the sanitation strike, recorded an announcement urging calm. But it didn't stop the rioting. The governor called in the state police and the Tennessee National Guard to control the streets. Black and white ministers pleaded with Mayor Henry Loeb to concede to the union's demands and end the strike. But the only action he took was to order a 7:00 PM curfew for the following evening.

The next morning the *New York Times* called Martin's murder "a disaster to the nation"; the *London Times*, "a great loss to the world." News of his death dominated the front page of the *Indiana Gazette* too, but Bobby's speech was buried on page four. His speech had only been broadcast on local television stations. Only those present the night before had experienced the power of Bobby's consoling words.

At noon in Cleveland, Ohio, Bobby called Martin's killing "a time of shame and sorrow. . . . We must recognize that this short life can neither be ennobled or enriched by hatred or revenge." He stood at the podium, eyes full of sorrow, urging, even begging the country to stop the violence. "Our lives on this planet are too short and the work to be done too great to let this spirit flourish any longer in our land."

News of Martin's assassination filled the headlines of newspapers across the world.

President Johnson attended a memorial service for King and then spoke to the nation, proclaiming April 7 a national day of mourning.

Mary Evans flew to Chicago to visit her grandmother over spring break. When she looked down at the city from the airplane window, she was startled to see plumes of smoke and fires on the South Side of Chicago. Altha Cravey had driven there with her family and was also shocked by the destruction in the streets.

With 46 dead, 4,600 injured, 20,000 arrested, and 70,000 troops and National Guardsmen on duty in cities across the land, many white Americans feared that the country was at war—with itself. They didn't understand why black people would destroy property and loot stores in their own communities.

Even black people who didn't support Martin's nonviolent protest methods had thought of him as their leader, their inspiration, and were devastated that he was gone.

On Saturday, April 6, four black servicemen from Mississippi and Tennessee sent Bobby a letter from Vietnam. "Why are we fighting the Viet Cong when back home our leader is killed? Why must we free the Vietnamese people when back home we do not have freedom?" They wished him luck in his presidential campaign "because we know that you will help everybody."

The next day, Bobby and Ethel, accompanied by Marian Wright, Peter Edelman, and a group of local officials, children, and citizens, walked through the riot-torn neighborhoods of Washington, DC. The stench of burning wood filled the air and broken glass covered the ground. But Bobby was not afraid. He wanted to witness the devastation for himself.

On Monday, April 8, Coretta and her four children led the march in Memphis in Martin's place. Forty-two thousand workers, community members, union leaders, entertainers, and supporters from all over the country, including Bobby and Ted Kennedy, walked the streets in silence, with only the sound of their shoes hitting the pavement. The calm and quiet were a balm to the violence on the streets of America's cities, and so different from the march 10 days earlier that had upset Martin so much. Coretta's composure, like Jackie Kennedy's five years earlier, inspired everyone.

In Atlanta that same day, 1,200 mourners an hour filed past Martin's casket in the sanctuary of his beloved Ebenezer Baptist Church. That night, after the King family returned to Atlanta, Bobby and Ethel visited their home to offer their condolences. No record exists of what was said, but Coretta welcomed their presence. At 3:00 AM, when the crowds had all gone home, John Lewis took the Kennedys to Ebenezer Baptist Church to quietly pay their respects to Martin.

The next morning hundreds of activists, entertainers, and national dignitaries crowded into Ebenezer Baptist Church for his funeral, while thousands waited outside and millions watched on television. For the second time in five years, the nation mourned together, just as they had during President Kennedy's funeral. Martin's best friend, Ralph Abernathy, gave the eulogy.

After the church service, Andy Young, Jesse Jackson, Jim Bevel, Hosea Williams, and the other pallbearers loaded Martin's coffin onto a flatbed farm truck pulled by two mules. A symbol of the Poor People's Campaign, it reminded the crowd of Martin's dream to bring thousands of poor people to Washington, DC, to lobby Congress.

A hundred thousand mourners followed the cart through the streets of Atlanta to Morehouse College, Martin's alma mater. Bobby and Ethel walked beside Charles Evers, the brother of slain civil rights activist Medgar Evers. Even now, after Martin's death, Bobby still had no security guards. He wanted to connect with people, especially the children who reached out to touch him. At Morehouse, Bobby was the only white person invited to sit on the platform during the second service in Martin's honor.

Afterward, he talked to one of Martin's associates and learned that Martin had a sense of humor. Bobby expressed sorrow that he had never gotten to know him on a personal basis. Only his family and close friends ever saw Martin's lighthearted side. As a Baptist minister, he believed he should be serious in public. Bobby liked to joke too. Perhaps if Martin had lived, humor could have eased some of the tension between them.

By 1968 they had come to respect each other but were still not friends. Martin approached civil rights with a fervent moral focus that seemed to pressure and confuse Bobby in the early days of the movement. When Bobby was no longer attorney general, they rarely met but closely followed each other's journeys through newspaper accounts and shared acquaintances. And now it was too late to deepen their relationship and work together.

Later that night Bobby met with Martin's closest associates. He wanted to know how his campaign could best honor Martin's legacy. Bitter and angry about their loss, they lashed out. Jim Bevel demanded to know if Bobby had a program to help them.

Bobby responded that he had some ideas but suggested that they get together at a later time. "I just came to pay tribute to a man that I had a lot of respect for."

Over the years, many of them had not trusted Bobby and had kept their distance. But when Bobby told them, "You have to pick up the torch of the cross of the fallen hero and carry it on. There's no slowing down, there's no stopping," Andy Young had a change of heart. "From that point on, I felt that this was a guy that I could give my life for, like I would have for Martin. I never felt that way about Gene McCarthy or [George] McGovern or anybody else."

After the meeting Hosea Williams admitted that someone in white America did care about black Americans. "King's murder left us hopeless, very desperate, dangerous men. I guess the thing that kept us going was that maybe Bobby Kennedy would come up with some answers for the country."

13

"WE STILL HAVE BOBBY KENNEDY"

In the weeks that followed Martin's death, black voters rallied behind Bobby, taking John Lewis's words to heart: "We still have Bobby Kennedy. We still have hope." They had lost their leader, but a candidate in the presidential race who understood their concerns helped eased their grief.

Journalist Jack Newfield traveled with the Kennedy campaign and believes that Martin's assassination altered Bobby's consciousness even more. It caused him "to glimpse the deeper roots of America's internal disease and imagine himself as the healer."

Bobby's campaign offered a template on how to run for president during a moral crisis when the nation desperately needed healing. He knew that he was privileged—a white male from a powerful, wealthy family. But he had come to realize that America's calling was to protect its most vulnerable people, just like Martin had so long preached.

He felt the need to lead the country even more now. A victory in Indiana's primary on May 8 was critical to winning the Democratic nomination. Eugene McCarthy led the delegate count, and soon Johnson's vice president, Hubert Humphrey, was expected to enter the race and would likely pick up support from Democratic delegates in states without primaries.

But Indiana was a challenge, a conservative state filled with blue-collar workers and few people of color. Talking about poverty was not popular. Even so, Bobby didn't change his tone or the content of his speeches to pander to voters. He told them what he truly believed. When poor whites and poor blacks turned out for his speeches, Bobby didn't talk down to them. He made them part of the conversation. Conservative voters appreciated how he favored civil rights but opposed disorder and the riots that had rocked cities across the land.

His campaign demonstrated what type of president he would be. He could be the missing link unifying blacks and working-class whites because he understood that everyone just wanted a job and a decent wage.

On April 23 he talked to a mixed crowd of students and local residents at Concordia College in Fort Wayne, Indiana. At first Bobby gave what he considered a dry speech about education reform, and then he spent 30 minutes talking about poverty. Afterward, the crowd gave him a standing ovation, but Bobby was still concerned that he had not moved them enough. He motioned for quiet and then said, "Camus once said there will always be suffering children in the world and if you and I don't help them, who will?" Then speaking in a whisper, he said, "Help us."

The crowd was so moved by Bobby's closing message that afterward they stood in silence instead of applauding.

On May 7 Bobby won the Indiana primary, carrying 41 percent of the vote with a coalition of blacks, students, and white blue-collar workers. He was on his way.

The SCLC followed Martin's wishes, naming Ralph Abernathy as his successor, and tried to move ahead with the Poor People's Campaign. In late April they released their "Statements of Demands for Rights of the Poor" to the press:

1. A meaningful job at a living wage for every employable citizen.
2. A secure and adequate income for all who cannot find jobs.
3. Access to land as a means to income and livelihood.
4. Access to capital as a means of full participation in the economic life of America.
5. Recognition by law of people affected by government programs to play a truly significant role in determining how they are designed and carried out.

Andy Young was impressed and grateful that Bobby and his staff supported the new protest when most national politicians were denouncing it. Andy said some black leaders avoided the Poor People's Campaign organizers "as if we were a contagious disease."

In early May, caravans departed from Virginia, Alabama, and Georgia, headed to Washington, DC, for the Poor People's Campaign. Demonstrators arrived by foot, car, bus, horse-drawn carriage, and mule train. On Mother's Day, May 12, Coretta Scott King led a march through the streets of the capital in support of the campaign. Ethel Kennedy marched too.

The following day 5,000 campers set up Resurrection City, a temporary settlement of tents and shacks on the National Mall. For six weeks protestors made pilgrimages to federal agencies and demonstrated at the offices of government officials, demanding more programs and funding for the poor.

Bobby won the Nebraska primary on May 14. But he lost in Oregon on May 28, in large part due to the antiwar college activists who supported McCarthy and the few voters of color who lived in the state. Next up was the California primary on June 5. Bobby told advisers that he would drop out of the race if he lost this all-important primary. But if he won, he'd try to make a deal with McCarthy, offering him the secretary of state position with a promise to end the war.

Bobby's supporters mobilized in huge numbers to help him win in America's largest and most diverse state. If Bobby won in California, it would demonstrate to Democratic Party leaders that he had enough support to win the national election. His dear friend Cesar Chavez, head of the National Farm Workers Association, led the effort to connect with Mexican American voters. Chavez had never forgotten Bobby's support of the 1965 Delano, California, grape boycott.

John Lewis and Charles Evers organized the outreach to black voters. Buoyed by a huge turnout and victories in black and Mexican American districts, along with the support of working-class whites, Bobby won the day.

That night thousands of supporters packed the ballroom in Los Angeles's Ambassador Hotel to celebrate. With Ethel by his side, Bobby again spoke to the crowd about what really mattered to him: "I think we can end the divisions in the United States . . . whether it's between blacks and whites, between the poor and the affluent, or between age groups, or over the war in Vietnam—that we can start to work together again. . . . So my thanks to all of you, and it's on to Chicago, and let's win there."

But right after midnight, as Bobby and Ethel took a shortcut through the hotel kitchen, Bobby was shot by a Palestinian refugee upset about Bobby's support of Israel. When the news spread, a campaign worker pounded a hotel pillar with his fist, crying out questions asked all around America that night: "Why, God, why? Why again? Why another Kennedy?"

At the hotel campaign headquarters, John Lewis dropped to his knees and sobbed.

After a four-hour surgery Bobby was stabilized, but his brain had ceased to function. America and the world awaited news of his condition. Twenty-five hours later, press secretary Frank Mankiewicz finally announced, "Robert Francis Kennedy died at 1:44 AM today, June 6, 1968. . . . He was forty-two years old."

Jackie Kennedy and Coretta Scott King accompanied Ethel Kennedy on the airplane carrying Bobby's body back to New York City.

"We loved him like a brother," Charles Evers said. "We lost the same thing when Bobby was killed that we lost when Jack was killed. We lost decency, unselfishness, leadership and concern for America. Jack. Bobby. Martin. Medgar. They were pioneers."

When Terri Alvies heard the news in Indianapolis, she wondered what the world was coming to. "We had really depended on the Kennedys to save us. With Dr. King gone, too, who would be our leader now?"

During the campaign, journalist Jack Newfield had lost the balanced view he needed as a reporter on Bobby's campaign beat and had fallen in love with Bobby and what he stood for. As he now mourned Bobby's death, he thought about a quote in Camus's book *Resistance, Rebellion and Death*: "A man does not show his greatness by being at one extremity, but rather by touching both at once." That was Bobby's great gift.

For two nights and a day, mourners waited for hours in the heat to pay their respects to Bobby, whose body was laid out in St. Patrick's Cathedral in New York City.

On June 8 Martin's murderer, James Earl Ray, was arrested at London's Heathrow Airport while trying to leave the United Kingdom with a false Canadian passport.

That same day Ted Kennedy gave the eulogy at his brother's funeral. Then Bobby's casket was loaded onto a 21-car train filled with family and friends for the trip to Washington, DC. Ethel sat in the caboose with Bobby's body and silently cried. Then she and her oldest son, Joe, walked through every train car, greeting friends and family.

All day long, white, black, and Latino mourners thronged both sides of the tracks as the train passed by. Boy Scouts, bridesmaids, firemen, housewives, children—one million people saluting, waving signs, crying, and shouting, "We miss you, Bobby. We love you."

Amateur photographer William F. Wisnom Sr., accompanied by his four grandchildren, took this photo of the huge crowd waiting for Bobby's train in Tullytown, Pennsylvania.

Americans were grieving Bobby, and Martin and JFK all over again. All three losses were so devastating that it was hard to imagine how the country would keep going and when the violence would end.

The trip usually took four hours, but eight hours later Bobby's funeral train arrived in Washington, DC, as darkness fell. As it traveled past Resurrection City on the National Mall, protestors stood and sang "We Shall Overcome."

Bobby was buried on a grass-covered hillside in Arlington Cemetery, 30 feet from his brother Jack. Words from his Indianapolis and South Africa speeches are etched on the flagstone surrounding his grave.

14

"SOMETHING DIED IN ALL OF AMERICA"

Bobby's death just two months after Martin's assassination catapulted the nation into another summer of violence. Americans, regardless of economic background or race, struggled to deal with the upheaval and the fear that came with the killing of two public leaders. No matter what they felt about Martin or Bobby, it seemed as if the fabric of the country were ripping apart.

Many young Americans found comfort in music that summer, by the Beatles, Bob Dylan, Aretha Franklin, Simon and Garfunkel, and other artists. One song honored the martyred leaders, linking Abraham Lincoln with three of the era's most influential voices. By fall it had reached the top of the charts. It wasn't a protest song, an anthem, or a gospel song, but more like a folk song that bridged all those styles of music and appealed to all ages and political beliefs. The song held no answers but offered solace to those mourning the recent deaths.

"Abraham, Martin and John"
By Dick Holler

Has anybody here seen my old friend Abraham?
Can you tell me where he's gone?
He freed a lot of people,
But it seems the good they die young.
You know, I just looked around and he's gone.

Anybody here, seen my old friend John?
Can you tell me where he's gone?
He freed a lot of people,
But it seems the good they die young.
I just looked around and he's gone.

Anybody here, seen my old friend Martin?
Can you tell me where he's gone?
He freed a lot of people,
But it seems the good they die young.
I just looked around and he's gone.

Didn't you love the things that they stood for?
Didn't they try to find some good for you and me?
And we'll be free
Some day, soon, it's gonna be one day

Anybody here, seen my old friend Bobby?
Can/won't you tell me where he's gone?
I thought I saw him walkin' up over the hill,
With Abraham, Martin and John.

For a month after Bobby's death, Eugene McCarthy canceled all campaign events and was kept under heavy security guard. He considered dropping out of the race, feeling guilty about veering away from his antiwar message and getting too personal in his attacks on Bobby during the Oregon and California primaries. Though his own passion had dimmed, antiwar activists persuaded him to stay in the race.

The Poor People's Campaign disbanded on June 24. Though far from reaching its goals, the protest produced some positive changes, such as additional funding for free and reduced lunches for schoolchildren, Head Start programs in Mississippi and Alabama, the expansion of food stamps, and streamlined welfare guidelines. Activists from different groups formed friendships and made plans to work together to address common issues, especially poverty.

The Kerner Report released in February had highlighted concerns over racist police practices, but the federal government failed to take any steps to address this institutional problem. With Martin gone, black power activists grew ever more vocal on issues like housing discrimination, policing, and unemployment.

Even the deaths of Martin and Bobby did not bring civility to the presidential campaign, and the atmosphere only worsened at the Democratic convention in Chicago in August 1968. Delegates defeated the peace plank in the party platform, even though 80 percent of primary voters had supported antiwar candidates Eugene McCarthy or Bobby Kennedy. Poverty was barely mentioned, with no acknowledgment of the Poor People's Campaign or Bobby's focus on it during his campaign. Afterward, some said the memorial film about Bobby Kennedy seemed to touch delegates more than any speech by a live politician.

The 10,000 peace activists protesting outside the convention hall and in local parks drew more press coverage than the speakers inside. Chicago mayor Richard J. Daley instructed city police to use any means necessary to control the protestors. During the convention police attacked more than 800 demonstrators, as a horrified nation once again watched the violence unfold on live television.

Protests exploded everywhere that fall, especially on college campuses, where thousands of students demonstrated against the war and discriminatory practices by university administrators. The women's movement protested the Miss America contest in September.

Thirty-two African nations boycotted the Summer Olympic Games in Mexico City in protest of South Africa's participation in spite of ongoing apartheid in that country. Plans for a protest by black Olympians had begun in November 1967 when US track and field athletes Tommie Smith and John Carlos participated in a group called the Olympic Project for Human Rights, which opposed apartheid as well as segregation and racism in general. In January 1968 Martin had publicly supported the group's efforts, but no organized boycott by the US team had taken place.

At their medal ceremony on October 17, however, Smith and Carlos, gold and bronze medalists in the 200-meter race, decided to protest injustice for African Americans by

Americans Smith and Carlos and Australian silver medalist Peter Norman also wore badges for the Olympic Project for Human Rights on their jackets during the ceremony.

doing the black power salute during the national anthem. At first the shocked crowd of 50,000 was silent. Then came boos, followed by people throwing things and screaming racial insults. The next day the International Olympic Committee cited the two runners for unsportsmanlike conduct and kicked them out of the athletes' village.

Years later Smith said, "I had a moral obligation to step up. Morality was a far greater force than the rules and regulations they had."

When peace talks in Paris stalled between the United States and North Vietnam, protests against the war escalated. On October 31 President Johnson announced a total halt to US bombing in North Vietnam. But it didn't help Hubert Humphrey in an already divisive general election campaign. Humphrey couldn't run against the war because he was Johnson's vice president and had supported LBJ's Vietnam policy. He focused his campaign on trying to find a path forward on Vietnam.

Republican nominee Richard Nixon, who had lost the presidency to John F. Kennedy in 1960, announced that he had a secret plan to end the war. But American troops did not withdraw from Vietnam for seven more years, until a 1975 peace treaty declared South and North Vietnam independent of each other.

Third-party candidate and white supremacist Alabama governor George Wallace encouraged violence at his campaign rallies, where his supporters often clashed with protestors. "The people know the way to stop a riot is to hit someone on the head," Wallace told reporters.

To appeal to the anxieties of white people, Nixon promised to increase policing and crack down on urban rioters. He called for the federal government to restore law and order throughout the nation. "Working Americans have become the forgotten Americans. In a time when the national rostrums and forums are given over to the shouters and protesters and demonstrators, they have become the silent Americans," Nixon said.

Nixon won by appealing to Americans who blamed the poor for their circumstances and who were frustrated and scared by all the student protests, the Black Panthers, antiwar marches, hippies, and feminists. Many young people were so disheartened by the violence and the political process that they stayed away from the polls. Humphrey ended up with only one percentage point fewer votes than Nixon. The support of Southern whites helped Wallace win 13 percent of votes and likely cost Humphrey the election. Surprisingly, many Wallace supporters in the general election had voted for Bobby in primary races. They thought both men would be tough on crime.

Would Bobby Kennedy have won the Democratic nomination and the general election? If so, what kind of president would he have been? These remain some of American history's big *what-if* questions. What is clear is that Bobby had broad appeal with voters and was ready for the job. "Bobby was the most prepared person to never serve as president," claims his biographer Larry Tye.

Historian William Pepper believes "that Bobby might have reached out . . . and tried to take Martin King on as a running mate. So, they could even have broadened their relationship."

It's unlikely that Martin would have agreed to run as vice president or that the country was ready for a black candidate. But if Bobby had won, Martin certainly would have advised him on many issues, especially poverty and race, and their journey would have continued.

At the end of 1968, Americans were even more divided and worried about the direction of their country. John Lewis may have said it best: "Something died in all of America in 1968. The sense of hope, of optimism, of *possibility* was replaced by horror, the worst of times, the feeling that maybe, just maybe, we would *not* overcome. . . . The question now, for both me and the country, was could we pick ourselves up yet again?"

EPILOGUE

"AMERICA IS NOT YET FINISHED"

"A man may die, nations may rise and fall, but an idea lives on," President John F. Kennedy said in a speech nine months before his death. Martin's and Bobby's ideas—to end poverty, stop an unjust war, show compassion to all Americans—will never go out of date. Their words have lived on, frequently quoted in blogs and articles and in speeches by modern activists and politicians. They continue to offer inspiration and insight on how the country can heal and face the historic challenges of economic and racial inequality.

In the months and years following their deaths, numerous streets, schools, and other public facilities were named after Bobby Kennedy and Martin Luther King. When Martin was killed, he had accomplished so much as the leader of the civil rights movement for 13 years, and today he remains a symbol of nonviolence across the world. He is the only nonpresident to have a national holiday and a monument on the National Mall in Washington, DC. Bobby is considered one of the finest attorney generals in America's history. The Justice Department building in Washington, DC, bears his name.

Since 1968 African Americans have begun breaking down the walls of prejudice in the fields of business, entertainment, and sports. Starting in the 1970s, black officials have been elected to positions in local, state, and federal governments. Shirley Chisholm ran for president in 1972, and Jesse Jackson in 1984 and 1988. Barack Obama, the first African American president, was elected in 2008, just seven years later than Bobby's 1961 prediction that a black president would be elected in 40 years. But even with great progress in all areas of American life and laws ending discrimination, racism still exists, and recent court decisions have eroded some of the legal protections.

The February 1968 Kerner Report identified police brutality against African Americans as a trigger for the rioting in cities across America. The federal government under President Richard Nixon did not take the necessary steps to combat this racism in the criminal justice system. Instead local police forces were militarized, more people were incarcerated for nonviolent crimes like drug possession, especially people of color, and more prisons were built to house them. Today 15 percent of black males go to prison at some point in their lifetime. The number of police shootings, especially of young black males, has skyrocketed.

The Black Lives Matter movement was started in July 2013 to protest the acquittal of George Zimmerman, who shot and killed black teen Trayvon Martin. The ongoing incidences of police violence and hate crimes by white people have sustained the movement. Black Lives Matter stands in solidarity with other current protest movements—immigrants' rights, gun control, the MeToo movement to end sexual harrassment of women, and the environment.

In September 2016 National Football League player Colin Kaepernick began protesting police shootings of black people by taking a knee during the national anthem. Other members of the NFL and athletes across the United

Several thousand protestors march in downtown Seattle in August 2017 to call attention to minority rights and police brutality.

States, both professional and amateur, have joined the protest. Americans are divided on whether such protests are
patriotic or un-American. The debate is similar to reac-
tions after track athletes Smith and Carlos's black power
salute at their 1968 Summer Olympics award ceremony.

Poverty has increased since 1968. Twenty percent of
American children now live in poverty, and 40 percent of
those are children of color. One percent of Americans owns
twice the wealth of the bottom 90 percent. Some historians believe that if President Johnson's War on Poverty programs had been fully funded in 1964, or were fully funded
today, America could wipe out poverty. Instead income
inequality has grown worse since Martin and Bobby spoke
so passionately about it in 1968.

Gun violence and the incidence of mass shootings continue to escalate. Since 1968 more people have died from
guns in the United States than during all the American
wars combined. In February 2018, a week after 17 students
and faculty were murdered in a mass shooting at Mar-
jory Stoneman Douglas High School in Parkland, Florida,
student leaders called on people to participate in March
for Our Lives protests around the country, to challenge
state and federal lawmakers to pass legislation to end the
bloodshed in schools and on the streets of American cities.
Thousands of supporters have joined their #NeverAgain
movement on social media. As Stoneman Douglas High
School freshman Christine Yared wrote in an editorial
in the *New York Times* on February 18, 2018, "We need to
work together beyond political parties to make sure this

never happens again. We need tougher gun laws. . . . We need to vote for those who are for stricter laws and kick out those who won't take action."

Passage of the 1964 Civil Rights Act and 1965 Voting Rights Act depended on the support and compromise of both Democrat and Republican legislators in Congress. But that did not happen until voters across the country demanded an end to segregation. A solution to gun violence calls for the same kind of political compromise. But the US Congress today has become so partisan and polarized that important issues like gun control have gotten bogged down by partisan quibbling and disputes. With little progress on issues like poverty, immigration, the national debt, and climate change, public confidence in our elected representatives has reached a new low.

There is little doubt that if Martin and Bobby were alive today both men would support the young people's movement and demand that Congress address the major problems facing Americans.

John Lewis did "pick himself up" after 1968 and has continued to work for change and fight injustice. He has served as Atlanta's representative in the House of Representatives since 1986. The last 1960s civil rights activist in Congress, Lewis is known as its moral voice. He has often said, "Whenever I have very tough decisions to make, I always think, 'What would Dr. King do? . . . What would Bobby Kennedy do?'"

Lewis encourages young people today to continue to take to the streets and stand up for what they believe. He is

heartened that students and people of all ages are protesting more than at any time since the 1960s.

Every year on April 4 the Indianapolis community
gathers to honor the 1968 night when America was sev-
ered in two, yet their city stood together. A young speaker
reenacts Martin's last speech, and a video of Bobby's brief
address is played. High school choirs sing, and student
speakers share their hopes for the future. Preachers plead
for people to renew their commitment to each other, and
politicians talk about how local groups can work together
to continue the legacy of both men.

In 1994 former Indiana secretary of state Larry Conrad
said, "Why don't we make a monument to peace where all
of us can live together, not with walls coming up but with
walls tearing down, so we can go forward together."

A ceremonial groundbreaking for the Landmark for
Peace memorial took place on May 14, 1994, attended by
President Bill Clinton, Senator Ted Kennedy, Ethel Kennedy, Dexter Scott King, and Martin Luther King III. On
September 30, 1995, the memorial was erected on the
exact spot where Bobby Kennedy had spoken 27 years
earlier. Indiana artist Greg Perry conceived and designed
the sculpture. It depicts Martin and Bobby reaching out
toward each other, Martin on the south end and Bobby on
the north end, with walls representing the history of each
man. Open sections with light shining through symbolize
their words that still resonate today.

"This is a place where a dream actually happened, where
violence was quelled, where a nonviolence philosophy

actually was realized," noted Kennedy King Memorial Initiative board member Judge David Dreyer.

The Kennedy King Memorial Initiative continues to build "on the historic events of April 4, 1968, by offering programs to raise awareness and inspire action to eliminate division and injustice." On March 23, 2018, Congress passed a bill naming the Kennedy King Memorial a National Commemorative Site.

Many who were at Bobby's speech on April 4 still live in the Broadway neighborhood of Indianapolis. College Club member Isaac Wilson was there. Today he and his wife own the Kountry Kitchen Soul Food Place, a restaurant only a few blocks from the Landmark for Peace memorial. Sometimes on election night local politicians, both Democrats and Republicans, gather at the restaurant, putting aside their differences for one night to talk about the old days and the future.

———— ★ ————

With political discord over immigration, medical care, and taxes, and ongoing protests over racism and police practices, America stands at another crossroads. In 1968 Martin and Bobby believed that ordinary citizens could recognize and deal with difficult challenges. They didn't have all the answers, but they kept trying.

Twenty-five years after their deaths, Coretta Scott King talked about how important it was not to mythologize Martin and Bobby. "What made these men great, however, was their humanness, the fact that their determination to make a difference is a resource that all people can call on," she said. "Those who lionize heroes do a disservice to the causes for which they stood. They create idols, who always have feet of clay."

At the 50th anniversary of the Selma march, President Obama, with Congressman John Lewis by his side, also spoke about how all people can make a difference. "When it comes to the pursuit of justice, we can afford neither complacency nor despair. There is no greater expression of faith in the American experiment than this; no greater form of patriotism is there than the belief that America is not yet finished," he said.

Recent national disasters—floods, hurricanes, earthquakes, and fires—have demonstrated Americans' willingness to help others in need. Martin and Bobby would applaud these efforts and urge us to continue to stand up for all people. It is wrong that children and adults go hungry in the richest nation on earth or that children are not safe in school or on the streets. It is right that every American be treated with dignity and respect.

AUTHOR'S NOTE

I was a teen in the 1960s and had a front-row seat to one of the most divisive and important decades in America's history. My parents were Democrats and we often discussed politics around the dinner table. When JFK won the 1960 presidential nomination, my brother John set up a campaign headquarters right in our home. I helped serve refreshments to the neighbors at a Kennedy tea hosted by my mother. My sister Mary Jo wore a pillbox hat, just like Jackie Kennedy. Like all of America, we were all devastated the day President Kennedy was killed.

My brother Jim had been killed that same year and like the Kennedys my siblings and I had been raised in the Catholic tradition to be strong and offer up suffering.

When Martin Luther King Jr. was killed five years later, a nun at my high school, Holy Names Academy, posted this message on the classroom bulletin board: CHRIST THE KING, KING THE CHRIST. Some of the students said it was sacrilegious to compare King to Jesus. But I thought it was brave and was grateful that Sister Margaret helped me think about Dr. King in such a radical way. Martin Luther King cared about the poor and disenfranchised, just like Jesus did in the gospel stories I'd grown up with.

My family closely followed the 1968 presidential election too. My brother John supported Eugene McCarthy because he spoke out first against the Vietnam War. I remember that my parents were shocked when Johnson withdrew from the race. Right after midnight on June 5, 1968, my mother shook me awake. "Get up, Claire. History is being made." Together we watched the chaos at the Ambassador Hotel in Los Angeles; the sobbing supporters had just learned that their candidate, Bobby Kennedy, had been gunned down in the hotel kitchen with Ethel by his side.

There was so much death and violence that year that I wondered how the country kept going. All summer I listened to the song "Abraham, Martin and John," with its last stanza featuring Bobby.

Decades passed. One evening I watched the documentary *A Ripple of Hope* about Robert Kennedy. Until then I had never heard Bobby's April 4 speech on the night of Martin Luther King Jr.'s assassination. Awed by the beauty of his words and the sorrow in his voice that touched the crowd so deeply, I had to learn more. I had to understand how and why Kennedy had such courage and was able to give such a powerful, healing speech on one of the worst days in America's history.

But I had so much to learn, so many people to talk to. Thousands of books, articles, blog posts, and documentaries feature King and Bobby Kennedy. I started with Harris Wofford's book *Of Kings and Kennedys* and kept reading until the day I completed my final revision of this book. I know so much more today about the 1960s and these two men who helped define that decade. But I wonder if any of us, participants or historians, can ever fully understand that complex era. One surprising fact I learned was that my brother John's dear friend Senator Maria Cantwell's father had stood behind Bobby that April night on the truck bed. Maria represents our state of Washington today because years ago her father Paul encouraged her to run for office.

In 2016 I attended the 48th commemoration of Dr. King's death and Bobby's speech at the Landmark for Peace memorial in Indianapolis. I am grateful to the many people who shared their vivid memories from that April night in 1968.

Author with John Lewis in his Washington, DC, congressional office.

In November 2014 I visited with Congressman John Lewis in Washington, DC. When I walked into his office, the walls covered with photos of Martin Luther King and Bobby Kennedy, and Lewis's many civil rights awards, I felt like I had entered a museum. We spent an hour together talking about that profound time and what King and Kennedy meant to him then and now.

Afterward I stood outside his office and cried. I had met my hero and he had given me hope. The words and efforts of Martin and Bobby live on in leaders like John Lewis, who not only inspire us but also remind us that the work for justice is never done. I am grateful that my work on this project has given me the opportunity to deeply study this important time and to reflect on what their words can teach us today about the need for compassion in our political dialogue and personal interactions.

ACKNOWLEDGMENTS

I am grateful to the many people who shared their insights and memories about Martin and Bobby and the 1960s. I thank Judge David Dreyer, board member of the Kennedy King Memorial Initiative in Indianapolis, who supported my visit to the 48th commemoration and connected me with many people. At the Indiana Historical Society, Eloise Baltic, Ray Boomhower, Amy Lamb, Dan Shockley, and librarian Wilma Gibbs Moore were most helpful with resources.

Thank you to my supportive family, especially my husband, who listened to many civil rights stories and watched my stack of books grow higher and higher. I thank my children, Conor and Megan; my son-in-law, Paul Gildea; and my grandson, Logan, who gives me hope for the future. Thank you to my sister Mary Jo and brother John for sharing their stories of the '60s and to the rest of my family for cheering me on during the long evolution of this project. I am grateful to my parents for instilling in us a love of reading, politics, and history, and the need to give back to our communities.

I am grateful for my writer friends Marilyn Carpenter, Mary Cronk Farrell, Mary Douthitt, Marsha Qualey, Meghan Sayres, and my writing community at Hamline University's MFAC program, and the faculty, students, and alums who listened to many excerpts and stories about my research, especially Ellen Kazimer. Personal friends Nancy Parker, Kathy Ely, Ann Waybright, Jane Parrish, and Mary and Wayne Ristau and so many others have stood by my side.

Finally, thank you to my editor Lisa Reardon for believing in this project, editor Ellen Hornor, and all those at Chicago Review Press who put their efforts and talents into producing this book.

TIME LINE

1925 November 20—Robert F. Kennedy is born in Brookline, Massachusetts.

1929 January 15—Martin Luther King Jr. is born in Atlanta, Georgia.

1948 MLK graduates from Morehouse College.
RFK graduates from Harvard University.

1951 RFK graduates from the University of Virginia law school.

1954 MLK becomes the pastor at Dexter Avenue Baptist Church in Montgomery, Alabama.

1955 MLK earns a doctorate in theology from Boston University.
December—Yearlong bus strike begins in Montgomery, Alabama; MLK is chosen as the leader of the strike.

1957 MLK is elected president of the Southern Christian Leadership Conference (SCLC).
RFK and JFK serve on the Senate Labor Rackets Committee.

1960 January—JFK declares his candidacy for president with RFK as campaign manager.
January—MLK moves to Atlanta, Georgia.
February—College students hold the first lunch counter sit-ins.
October 19—MLK is arrested at a lunch counter sit-in in Atlanta.
October 26—JFK calls Coretta and RFK calls a judge to discuss releasing MLK from jail.

October 27—MLK is released from Reidsville Prison.

November 8—JFK is elected the 35th president of the United States.

1961 January 20—JFK is inaugurated as 35th president of the United States.

January 21—JFK appoints RFK as attorney general.

May 4—Freedom Riders begin protesting segregation on Southern bus routes.

May 14—Freedom Riders are attacked in Anniston, Alabama.

May 21—Segregationists grow violent outside a Montgomery, Alabama, church while supporters pray inside.

November 1—Enforcement of ICC regulations ending segregation in interstate bus stations.

1963 May 2—Children's Crusade begins in Birmingham.

June 11—JFK announces civil rights legislation on television.

August 28—March on Washington for Jobs and Freedom is held; MLK gives his "I Have a Dream" speech.

September 15—Four black girls are killed at a Birmingham church by a bomb planted by the Ku Klux Klan.

November 22—JFK is killed in Dallas; Lyndon Baines Johnson is sworn in as the new president.

1964 July 2—LBJ signs the Civil Rights Act.

September—RFK resigns as attorney general and declares candidacy for New York Senate seat.

November 3—RFK is elected senator from New York; LBJ is elected president.

December—MLK is awarded the Nobel Peace Prize.

1965 March 7—Protestors for voting rights are attacked on Edmund Pettus Bridge in Selma, Alabama.

March 8—LBJ sends first US combat troops to Vietnam.

August 6—LBJ signs the Voting Rights Act.

August 11—Riots break out in the Watts neighborhood of Los Angeles, California.

1966 June—RFK visits South Africa and speaks out against apartheid.

1967 March 2—RFK speaks out against the Vietnam War on the Senate floor.

April 4—MLK speaks out against the Vietnam War at Riverside Church in New York City.

April 10—RFK tours the Mississippi delta region to study poverty issues.

July—Riots erupt in Newark and Detroit; LBJ appoints the Kerner Commission to investigate the causes.

December 4—MLK and the SCLC announce the Poor People's Campaign.

1968 February 29—Kerner Commission issues its report on the riots.

March 16—RFK declares his candidacy for president.

March 18—MLK speaks in Memphis to an enthusiastic crowd; RFK gives his first presidential campaign speeches to enthusiastic crowds in Kansas.

March 28—MLK leads a Memphis march that turns violent.

March 31—LBJ announces he will not run for reelection.

April 3—MLK gives his final speech at Mason Temple in Memphis.

April 4—MLK is killed in Memphis; RFK speaks in Indianapolis.

May 7—RFK wins Indiana Democratic primary.

May 12—On Mother's Day, Coretta Scott King leads a march in Washington, DC, to launch the Poor People's Campaign; Resurrection City set up.

May 28—Eugene McCarthy wins the Oregon Democratic primary.

June 5—RFK wins the California primary and is shot after the rally.

June 6—RFK dies in Los Angeles.

June 24—Poor People's Campaign ends.

November 5—Nixon wins the presidential election over Democrat Hubert Humphrey.

1986 First MLK holiday is celebrated on the third Monday in January.

1995 September 30—Landmark for Peace memorial is dedicated in Indianapolis's Dr. Martin Luther King Jr. Park.

PLACES TO VISIT, IN PERSON OR ONLINE

___

The Center for Civil and Human Rights
www.civilandhumanrights.org

John F. Kennedy Presidential Library and Museum
www.jfklibrary.org

The Kennedy King Memorial Initiative
www.kennedykingindy.org

LBJ Presidential Library
www.discoverlbj.org

The Martin Luther King Jr. Center for Nonviolent Social Change
www.thekingcenter.org

National Civil Rights Museum at the Lorraine Motel
www.civilrightsmuseum.org

Smithsonian National Museum of African American
   History and Culture
https://nmaahc.si.edu

National Voting Rights Museum and Institute
www.nvrmi.com

Robert F. Kennedy Human Rights
www.rfkcenter.org

NOTES

Prologue: "What Kind of a Nation We Are"

"I have sad news for you": Robert F. Kennedy, "Remarks on the Assassination of Martin Luther King Jr.," April 4, 1968, http://americanrhetoric.com/speeches/rfkonmlkdeath.html.

"what kind of a nation": Kennedy, "Remarks on the Assassination."

Chapter 1: "I Think We Can Do Better"

"Ladies and gentleman": Ralph David Abernathy, *And the Walls Came Tumbling Down: An Autobiography* (New York: Harper and Row, 1989), 428.

"would make a great president": David J. Garrow, *Bearing the Cross: Martin Luther King, Jr., and the Southern Christian Leadership Conference* (New York: William Morrow, 1986), 576.

"Our nation is moving toward two societies": US Department of Justice, "Report of the National Advisory Commission on Civil Disorders," February 20, 1981, www.ncjrs.gov/pdffiles1/Digitization/8073NCJRS.pdf.

"This country needs honesty and candor" through *"I don't think"*: Robert F. Kennedy, "Remarks at the University of Kansas, March 18, 1968," www.jfklibrary.org/Research/Research-Aids/Ready-Reference/RFK-Speeches/Remarks-of-Robert-F-Kennedy-at-the-University-of-Kansas-March-18-1968.aspx.

"I want everybody to get together": Taylor Branch, *At Canaan's Edge: America in the King Years, 1965–68* (New York: Simon and Schuster, 2007), 750.

Chapter 2: "I've Been to the Mountaintop"

How quickly can I get there?: Johnnie Turner, interview by author, May 2016.

"You are demonstrating": "Memphis Sanitation Workers Strike (1968)," Martin Luther King Jr. and the Global Freedom Struggle website, http://kingencyclopedia.stanford.edu/encyclopedia /encyclopedia/enc_memphis_sanitation_workers_strike_1968.

"Martin, the people who are": Abernathy, *And the Walls*, 431–432.

"but he is the one": Branch, *Canaan's Edge*, 756.

"We aren't going to let dogs": Martin Luther King Jr., "I've Been to the Mountaintop," April 3, 1968, www.americanrhetoric.com /speeches/mlkivebeentothemountaintop.htm.

"Dear Dr. King": Margalit Fox, "Izola Ware Curry, Who Stabbed King in 1958, Dies at 98," *New York Times*, March 21, 2015, www .nytimes.com/2015/03/22/us/izola-ware-curry-who-stabbed -king-in-1958-dies-at-98.html.

"We've got some difficult days ahead": King, "Mountaintop."

"I may not get there": King, "Mountaintop."

Chapter 3: "What We Really Stand For"

"This is the most affluent nation": Thurston Clarke, *The Last Campaign: Robert F. Kennedy and the 82 Days That Inspired America* (New York: Henry Holt, 2008), 84.

"I've just come": Jack Hayes, Barbara Maddix, Sasha Nyary, Steven Petrow, and Denise L. Stinson, "What Did We Lose?" *Life*, April 1993, 59.

"If this country amounts to anything now": Ray E. Boomhower, *Robert F. Kennedy and the 1968 Indiana Primary* (Indianapolis: Indiana University Press, 2008), 59.

"She's always happy": Branch, *Canaan's Edge*, 761.

"Indiana, are you ready": Clarke, *Last Campaign*, 85.

"Here in America": Robert F. Kennedy, "Primary Campaign Address at Ball State University," April 4, 1968, http://libx.bsu.edu/cdm /singleitem/collection/RFKen/id/22.

"The American people should": Kennedy, "Ball State."

"He's perfectly entitled to": Boomhower, *Indiana Primary*, 60.

"Your speech implies": Boomhower, 60.

"Doc, you remember": Taylor Branch, *The King Years: Historic Moments in the Civil Rights Movement* (New York: Simon and Schuster, 2013), 183–184.

Chapter 4: "When Is This Violence Going to Stop?"

"You ought to be dead": Jane Hedeen, Michael Hutchison, and Brenda Kreiger, "The Issue of Race in 1968: A Case Study of the Broadway Neighborhood," Indiana Historical Society curriculum guide, 2011, 16–17, https://indianahistory.org/wp-content/uploads/83a052891688239137694d81159b01af.pdf.

LET'S SEND LIGHT BACK TO THE WHITES: Hedeen, Hutchison, and Kreiger, "Issue of Race."

"Civil rights leader": "Martin Luther King Jr. Shot—CBS Radio News First Report," www.youtube.com/watch?v=cefI3Fw51bA.

"We just got word": David Levering Lewis, *King: A Biography*, 3rd ed. (Urbana: University of Illinois Press, 2013), 386.

"Then they'll walk if they have to": Mike Riley, interview by author, April 2016.

"Have you heard about Martin Luther King?": Boomhower, *Indiana Primary*, 3.

"sagged" and *"his eyes went blank"*: Evan Thomas, "The Worst Week of 1968," *Newsweek*, November 10, 2007, www.newsweek.com/worst-week-1968-96797.

"To think that I just finished": David Halberstam, *The Unfinished Odyssey of Robert Kennedy* (New York: Random House, 1968), 85.

"Give a very short speech": Frank Mankiewicz and Joel L. Swerdlow, *So As I Was Saying . . . : My Somewhat Eventful Life* (New York: Thomas Dunne Books, 2016), 179.

"I know what Mrs. King": Clarke, *Last Campaign*, 89.

"He's going": Abernathy, *And the Walls*, 443.

"Dr. Martin Luther King Jr": "Radio Coverage of the Assassination of Dr. Martin Luther King, Jr," WCCO Radio, www.youtube.com/watch?v=fBc4pRpwPaQ.

Her place was with them: Stephen B. Oates, *Let the Trumpet Sound: A Life of Martin Luther King., Jr.* (New York: Harper Perennial, 2013), 493.

"Oh, God": Clarke, *Last Campaign*, 89.

Chapter 5: "To Whom Much Is Given, Much Is Asked"

"We don't want any losers": Arthur M. Schlesinger Jr., *Robert Kennedy and His Times* (Boston: Houghton Mifflin, 1978), 14.

"Attacking the game": Schlesinger, 43.

"He didn't care": William Plummer, "RFKennedy: Bobby, as We Knew Him," *People*, June 6, 1988, http://people.com/archive/rfkennedy-bobby-as-we-knew-him-vol-29-no-22.

"They were like sports": Marc Aronson, *Up Close: Robert F. Kennedy* (New York: Viking Juvenile, 2007), 44.

"This is a boy": Richard Lischer, *Martin Luther King Jr. and the Word That Moved America* (New York: Oxford University Press, 1995), 6.

"believing that if you had": Lischer, 40.

"My heart throbs anew": Martin Luther King Jr., "The Negro and the Constitution," May 1–31, 1944, https://kinginstitute.stanford.edu/king-papers/documents/negro-and-constitution.

"It was the angriest": Clayborne Carson, ed., *The Autobiography of Martin Luther King, Jr.* (New York: Warner Books, 2001), 10.

Chapter 6: "Until Justice Runs Down Like Water"

"If I can be of service": Oates, *Let the Trumpet Sound*, 68–69.

"We are determined": Martin Luther King Jr., "The Montgomery Bus Boycott," December 5, 1955, www.blackpast.org/1955-martin-luther-king-jr-montgomery-bus-boycott.

Beloved Community: "The King Philosophy," King Center website, www.thekingcenter.org/king-philosophy.

"I don't know what Bobby does": George W. Bush, "Remarks by the President at Dedication of the Robert F. Kennedy Department of Justice Building," November 20, 2001, https://georgewbush-whitehouse.archives.gov/news/releases/2001/11/20011120-15.html.

"Nobody asked me": John F. Kennedy, *The Letters of John F. Kennedy*, ed. Martin W. Sandler (New York: Bloomsbury Press, 2015), 43.

"We're in trouble with Negroes": Alex Poinsett, *Walking with Presidents: Louis Martin and the Rise of Black Political Power* (Lanham, MD: Madison Books, 1997), 62.

"He had never": Carson, ed., *Autobiography*, 144.

"Do you know that three": Harris Wofford, *Of Kennedys and Kings: Making Sense of the Sixties* (New York: Farrar, Strauss and Giroux, 1980), 19.

"If you are a decent American": Wofford, *Kennedys and Kings*, 21.

"I am deeply indebted": Poinsett, *Walking with Presidents*, 85.

"Negro whose name": Branch, *King Years*, 24.

Chapter 7: "The Time Has Come for This Nation to Fulfill Its Promise"

"Let the word go forth": John F. Kennedy, "President Kennedy's Inaugural Address," January 20, 1961, www.jfklibrary.org/Research/Research-Aids/Ready-Reference/JFK-Quotations/Inaugural-Address.aspx.

"As long as you're in church": Taylor Branch, *Parting the Waters: America in the King Years 1954–63* (New York: Simon and Schuster, 1988), 460.

"You must understand": Garrow, *Bearing the Cross*, 160.

"Somewhere in this man sits good": Larry Tye, "The Most Trusted White Man in Black America," *Politico Magazine*, July 7, 2016, www.politico.com/magazine/story/2016/07/robert-f-kennedy-race-relations-martin-luther-king-assassination-214021.

"ungodly actions": Martin Luther King Jr., "Letter from a Birmingham Jail," April 16, 1963, www.africa.upenn.edu/Articles_Gen/Letter_Birmingham.html.

"Injustice anywhere is a threat to justice everywhere": King, "Birmingham Jail."

"What if this": David Gruber, *RFK: American Experience* (PBS, 2004).

"sick": Jonathon Rieder, *Gospel of Freedom: Martin Luther King, Jr.'s Letter from Birmingham Jail and the Struggle That Changed a Nation* (New York: Bloomsbury Press, 2013), 131.

"The children have been suffering": *The March: The Story of the Greatest March in American History* (Smoking Dogs Films U.K., 2013).

"He was attorney general": Hayes et al., "What Did We Lose?" 65.

"President Kennedy must begin": Branch, *King Years*, 54.

"The heart of the question": John F. Kennedy, "Report to the American People on Civil Rights," June 11, 1963, www.jfklibrary.org/Asset-Viewer/LH8F_0Mzv0e6Ro1yEm74Ng.aspx.

Chapter 8: "I Have a Dream"

"We have demanded": Gordon Brown, *Courage: Portraits of Bravery in the Service of Great Causes* (New York: Weinstein Books, 2008), 111.

"The young people": John Lewis, with Michael D'Orso, *Walking with the Wind: A Memoir of the Movement* (New York: Harcourt Brace, 1998), 213.

"Martin Luther King, the moral leader": *The March: The Story of the Greatest March in American History* (Smoking Dogs Films U.K., 2013).

"I have a dream": Martin Luther King Jr., "I Have a Dream," 1963, www.archives.gov/files/press/exhibits/dream-speech.pdf.

"One of the best speeches": Branch, *Parting the Waters*, 883.

"glad to be standing": Edith Lee-Payne, "Finding the Girl in the Photograph," *The National Archives Pieces of History* (blog), October 16, 2011, https://prologue.blogs.archives.gov/2011/10/16/finding-the-girl-in-the-photograph.

"the Kennedy and Johnson Administrations": David J. Garrow, "The FBI and Martin Luther King," *Atlantic*, July/August 2002, www.theatlantic.com/magazine/archive/2002/07/the-fbi-and-martin-luther-king/302537.

"You see him being intensely": Jen Christensen, "FBI Tracked King's Every Move," CNN, December 29, 2008, www.cnn.com/2008/US/03/31/mlk.fbi.conspiracy/index.html?_s=PM:US.

"President Kennedy died": "JFK assassination: Cronkite informs a shocked nation," www.youtube.com/watch?v=6PXORQE5-CY.

"Corrie, this is what is going to happen": Coretta Scott King, *My Life with Martin Luther King, Jr.* (New York: Holt, Rinehart, and Winston, 1969), 227.

"Uncle Jack had the most": Larry Tye, *Bobby Kennedy: The Making of a Liberal Icon* (New York: Random House, 2016), 285.

"It was as though he had lost": Rory Kennedy, *Ethel* (HBO documentary, Warner Bros. Entertainment Inc., 2013).

"He who learns must suffer": Duane W. Krohnke, "Aeschylus on Suffering and Wisdom," *dwkcommentaries* (blog), February 10, 2014, https://dwkcommentaries.com/2014/02/10/aeschylus-on -suffering-and-wisdom.

Chapter 9: "A Tiny Ripple of Hope"

"He was our partner in crime": Hayes et al, "What Did We Lose?" 59.

"We shall overcome": Lyndon B. Johnson, "Voting Rights Act Address," March 15, 1965, www.greatamericandocuments.com /speeches/lbj-voting-rights.

"We've got to see that": Wofford, *Kennedys and Kings*, 321.

"that have created Negro frustrations": Schlesinger, *Robert Kennedy*, 779.

"Northern problems are": Scott Martelle, "Viewing the Watts Riots Through Different Eyes," *Los Angeles Times*, August 12, 2015, www.latimes.com/opinion/opinion-la/la-ol-watts-reactions -kennedy-king-johnson-eisenhower-20150810-story.html.

"He's right, Andy": Andrew Young, *An Easy Burden: The Civil Rights Movement and the Transformation of America* (New York: Harper-Collins, 1996), 380.

"But Martin took it": Young, *Easy Burden*, 380.

"Each time a man stands up": Robert F. Kennedy, "Day of Affirmation Address at Cape Town University," June 6, 1966, www .americanrhetoric.com/speeches/rfkcapetown.htm.

"A nation that continues": Wofford, *Kings and Kennedys*, 424.

"The only way there's": Schlesinger, *Robert Kennedy*, 873.

"Now I know how": Jack Newfield, *RFK: A Memoir* (New York: Nation Books, 2003), 72.

Chapter 10: "Do They Know About Martin Luther King?"

"You can't have a crowd like this come": Lewis, *Walking with the Wind*, 386.

"There's no way": Robert F. Kennedy quoted in Daniel T. Miller, *A Tragic Turn: Six Leaders and the Death of Martin Luther King, Jr.* (Bloomington, IN: AuthorHouse, 2008), 41.

"I can't protect you, Senator" through *"You know what to say"*: Donald Boggs, *A Ripple of Hope* (Anderson, IN: Covenant Productions, Anderson University, 2010).

They're going to burn down the city: Darlene Howard, interview by author, April 2016.

"He's on his way" through *"I'm sorry, John"*: Lewis, *Walking with the Wind*, 386.

"King didn't deserve": Karl W. Anatol and John R. Bittner, "Kennedy on King: The Rhetoric of Control," *Today's Speech* 16, no. 3 (1968): 32.

"like the blood": JoMarva Bell, interview by author, August 2013.

"It was like he wasn't there": Boggs, *Ripple of Hope*.

"Do they know?": Boggs, *Ripple of Hope*.

Chapter 11: "I Have Some Very Sad News for All of You"

All RFK speech quotes in this chapter from Kennedy, "Remarks on the Assassination."

"Who killed Dr. King?": Anatol and Bittner, "Kennedy on King."

Like a gnat on cotton: Darlene Howard, interview by author, April 2016.

It was as if the senator: Mary Evans, interview by author, February 2016.

"It's the thirteenth birthday": JoMarva Bell, interview by author, August 2013.

"He didn't talk down to us": Billie Breaux, interview by author, June 2013.

Chapter 12: "A Time of Shame and Sorrow"

"Big business is trying": Boomhower, *Indiana Primary*, 69.

"completely sympathetic and understanding": Tye, "Most Trusted White Man."

"a disaster to the nation": Oates, *Let the Trumpet Sound*, 494.

"a great loss to the world": Oates, 494.

"a time of shame and sorrow": Mankiewicz and Swerdlow, *So As I Was Saying*, 184.

"Why are we fighting the Viet Cong": Joseph A. Palermo, *In His Own Right: The Political Odyssey of Senator Robert F. Kennedy* (New York: Columbia University Press, 2001), 183.

"*I just came to pay tribute*": Schlesinger, *Robert Kennedy*, 879.
"*You have to pick up*": Young, *Easy Burden*, 486.
"*King's murder left us hopeless*": Schlesinger, *Robert Kennedy*, 879.

Chapter 13: "We Still Have Bobby Kennedy"

"*We still have Bobby Kennedy*": Lewis, *Walking With the Wind*, 393.
"*to glimpse the deeper roots*": Newfield, *RFK*, 57.
"*Camus once said*": Clarke, *Last Campaign*, 180.
"*Statements of Demands for Rights of the Poor*": Southern Christian Leadership Conference, "Statements of Demands for the Rights of the Poor," April 29–30, May 1, 1968, 2, www.crmvet.org/docs /6805_ppc_demands.pdf.
"*as if we were a contagious disease*": Young, *Easy Burden*, 486.
"*I think we can end*": Joe Allen, "The Bobby Kennedy Myth," SocialistWorker.org, June 6, 2008, http://socialistworker. org/2008/06/06/bobby-kennedy-myth.
"*Why, God, why?*": Tye, *Bobby Kennedy*, 473.
"*Robert Francis Kennedy*": Tye, 473.
"*We loved him*": Plummer, "RFKennedy."
"*We had really depended*": Terri Glover, interview by author, April 2016.
"*A man does not*": Newfield, *RFK*, 304.
"*We miss you, Bobby*": Tye, *Bobby Kennedy*, 439.

Chapter 14: "Something Died in All of America"

"*Has anybody here seen my old friend Abraham?*": "Abraham, Martin and John" lyrics, rights by Regent Music Corporation, www.metrolyrics.com/abraham-martin-and-john-lyrics-dion .html.
"*I had a moral obligation*": Popspotted, "MLK 50th: Dr. Martin Luther King Impact on John Carlos and 1968 Olympic Protest," POPSspot, August 22, 2013, www.popsspot.com/2013/08/mlk -50th-dr-martin-luther-king-impact-on-john-carlos-and-1968 -olympic-protest.
"*The people know the way*": Peter Beinart, "The Violence to Come," *Atlantic*, March 3, 2016, www.theatlantic.com/politics/archive /2016/03/the-violence-to-come/471924.

"Working Americans have become": Beinart, "Violence to Come."

"Bobby was the most prepared": Tye, *Bobby Kennedy*, 397

"that Bobby might have reached out": William F. Pepper, interview on *Project Censored* radio show, April 7, 2017, https://kpfa.org/episode/project-censored-april-7-2017.

"Something died in all of America": Lewis, *Walking With the Wind*, 401.

Epilogue: "America Is Not Yet Finished"

"A man may die": John F. Kennedy, "Remarks Recorded for the Opening of a USIA Transmitter at Greenville, North Carolina," February 8, 1963 www.presidency.ucsb.edu/ws/?pid=9551.

"We need to work": Christine Yared, "Don't Let My Classmates' Deaths Be in Vain," *New York Times*, February 18, 2018, www.nytimes.com/2018/02/18/opinion/florida-school-shooting-guns.html.

"Whenever I have very tough decisions": John Lewis, "John Lewis Tells His Truth About 'Selma,'" *Los Angeles Times*, January 17, 2015, www.latimes.com/nation/la-oe-lewis-selma-movie-20150119-story.html.

"Why don't we make a monument": "The Park," Kennedy King Memorial Initiative website, http://kennedykingindy.org/the-park.

"This is a place": Diana Penner, "Building on a Dream," *Indianapolis Star*, March 30, 2009.

"on the historic events": "Our Mission," Kennedy King Memorial Initiative website, http://kennedykingindy.org/the-initiative.

"What made these men great": Hayes et al., "What Did We Lose?" 59.

"When it comes to the pursuit of justice": Barack Obama, "Remarks by the President at the 50th Anniversary of the Selma to Montgomery Marches," March 7, 2015, https://obamawhitehouse.archives.gov/the-press-office/2015/03/07/remarks-president-50th-anniversary-selma-montgomery-marches.

BIBLIOGRAPHY

Visit the author's website for a complete list of sources used in the research of the book and suggestions for further study: www.clairerudolfmurphy.com.

Titles below with an asterisk are especially suitable for young readers.

Books

Abernathy, Ralph David. *And the Walls Came Tumbling Down: An Autobiography*. New York: Harper and Row, 1989.

Boomhower, Ray E. *Robert F. Kennedy and the 1968 Indiana Primary*. Indianapolis: Indiana University Press, 2008.

Branch, Taylor. *At Canaan's Edge: America in the King Years, 1965–68*. New York: Simon and Schuster, 2007.

*Branch, Taylor. *The King Years: Historic Moments in the Civil Rights Movement*. New York: Simon and Schuster, 2013.

Branch, Taylor. *Parting the Waters: America in the King Years 1954–63*. New York: Simon and Schuster, 1988.

Carson, Clayborne, ed. *The Autobiography of Martin Luther King, Jr.* New York: Warner Books, 2001.

Clarke, Thurston. *The Last Campaign: Robert F. Kennedy and the 82 Days That Inspired America*. New York: Henry Holt, 2008.

Garrow, David J. *Bearing the Cross: Martin Luther King, Jr., and the Southern Christian Leadership Conference*. New York: William Morrow, 1986.

Lewis, John, with Michael D'Orso. *Walking with the Wind: A Memoir of the Movement*. New York: Harcourt Brace, 1998.

Newfield, Jack. *RFK: A Memoir*. New York: Nation Books, 2003.

Oates, Stephen B. *Let the Trumpet Sound: A Life of Martin Luther King, Jr.* New York: Harper Perennial, 2013.

Schlesinger, Arthur M., Jr. *Robert Kennedy and His Times*. Boston: Houghton Mifflin, 1978.

Tye, Larry. *Bobby Kennedy: The Making of a Liberal Icon*. New York: Random House, 2016.

Wofford, Harris. *Of Kennedys and Kings: Making Sense of the Sixties*. New York: Farrar, Strauss and Giroux, 1980.

Young, Andrew. *An Easy Burden: The Civil Rights Movement and the Transformation of America*. New York: HarperCollins, 1996.

Magazine, Newspaper, and Online Articles

Anatol, Karl W., and John R. Bittner. "Kennedy on King: The Rhetoric of Control." *Today's Speech* 16, no. 3 (1968): 31–34.

Hayes, Jack, Barbara Maddix, Sasha Nyary, Steven Petrow, and Denise L. Stinson, "What Did We Lose?" *Life*, April 1993.

Plummer, William. "RFKennedy: Bobby, as We Knew Him." *People*. June 6, 1988. http://people.com/archive/rfkennedy-bobby-as-we-knew-him-vol-29-no-22.

Speeches

Kennedy, Robert F. "Remarks on the Assassination of Martin Luther King, Jr." April 4, 1968. http://americanrhetoric.com/speeches/rfkonmlkdeath.html.

King, Martin Luther, Jr. "I've Been to the Mountaintop." April 3, 1968. www.americanrhetoric.com/speeches/mlkivebeentothemountaintop.htm.

Video

Boggs, Donald. *A Ripple of Hope* (Anderson, IN: Covenant Productions, Anderson University, 2010).

The March: The Story of the Greatest March in American History (Smoking Dogs Films U.K., narrated by Denzel Washington, 2013).

Interviews by Author

JoMarva Bell, August 2013 and April 2016 (telephone).

Billie Breaux, June 2013 (telephone) and April 2016 (in person).

Jean Breaux, June 2013 (telephone) and April 2016 (in person).

Rev. Tom Brown, April 2016 (telephone).

Ed Burke, November 2016 (telephone and in person).

Senator Maria Cantwell, April 2013 (in person).

Rose Cantwell, May 2013 (telephone).

Altha Carey, August 2013 (telephone and email).

Mary Evans, February 2016 (telephone).

Terri Alvies Glover, April 2016 (telephone).

Willie Wilbert Herenton, July 2016 (telephone).

Mark Higbee, October 2013 (telephone).

Aleta Hodge, July 2016 (telephone).

Darlene Howard, April 2016 (telephone).

John Lewis, November 2014 (in person).

Wilma Gibbs Moore, April 2016 (telephone).

Loraine Minor Morris, May 2016 (telephone).

Greg Perry, April 2016 (in person).

Rutha Powell, August 2013 (telephone).

Michael Riley, April 2016 (telephone).

Abie Robinson, April 2016 (telephone).

Harry Rogers, June 2016 (telephone).

Jim Trulock, April 2016 (in person).

Johnnie R. Turner, May 2016 (telephone).

Isaac Wilson, April 2016 (in person).

IMAGE CREDITS

Page viii: Photo by D. Todd Moore, University of Indianapolis staff photographer

Page 2: Photo by Ron Reister/photoshelter

Page 8: Courtesy of Bentley Historical Library, University of Michigan, Jay Cassidy photograph collection 1967–1970, RFK_68016_017

Page 12: AP Images, File 630412024

Page 23: AP Images- file 680403048, photo by Charles Kelly

Page 34: Courtesy of the John F. Kennedy Library Foundation, KFC1239P

Page 42: AP Images - file 48010101635

Page 49: Courtesy of the Library of Congress, LC-USZ62-135494

Page 54: AP Images - file 601027059, photo by Beaumont

Page 57: Courtesy of Library of Congress, LC-USF33-20522-M2

Page 64: AP Images, photo by Bill Hudson

Page 69: John F. Kennedy Presidential Library and Museum, AR7993-B

Page 71: Courtesy National Archives and Records Administration, no. 306-SSM-4C-61-32, photo by Rowland Scherman

Page 79: Courtesy of Library of Congress, LC-USZ62-133299, photo by Dick DeMarsico

Page 94: Indiana Recorder Collection, Indiana Historical Society, PO 303

Page 98: Courtesy of Jim Trulock

Page 104: AP Images - file 6804051784
Page 115: Photo by William F. Wisnom, Sr., courtesy of Leslie
    Dawson
Page 121: AP Images - file 16268128268630
Page 127: Alex Menendez, AP Images
Page 135: Photo by Ellen Kazimer

INDEX

Howard, Darlene, 92, 97, 99, 101
Humphrey, Hubert, 77, 110, 122–123

Indiana
    Indianapolis, 25–28
    RFK campaigning in, 18–19, 21–24, 110, 111
Indiana Gazette, 103
Interstate Commerce Commission (ICC), 60

Jackson, Jesse, 10, 17, *23*, 24, 65–66, 107, 126
Jim Crow laws, 40, 46
    See also segregation
Johnson, Lyndon Baines, 4–6, 9, 50, *69*, 74–76, 81, 85, 88, 122

Kaepernick, Colin, 127
Kennedy, Ethel, 5, 7, 24, 30, 48, 75, 90, 113, 130
Kennedy, Jack. *See* Kennedy, John F.
Kennedy, Jackie, 114
Kennedy, John F., 5, 9, 31, 35–37, *49*, 50, 53, 55, 65–66, 70–71, 73–74, 85, 114, 116, 125
Kennedy, Joseph, *33–35*, 55
Kennedy, Joseph, Jr., *34*, 35
Kennedy, Robert F. "Bobby," 4–5, 18–19, 33, *34*, 35–36, *69*, *79*, 82–83, 123
    and DC riots, 105–106

family, 48, 101
funeral, 115
funeral train, *115*, 116
government committees, 48–49, *49*
interactions with King, 53, 58, 65, 69–70, 72–73, 107–108
and JFK's death, 74–76, 99
at King's funeral, 106–107
and King's shooting, 30, 32, 90–94, *94*, 96, 99–101, 103–104
political campaigns, 6–7, *8*, 14, 19–24, 26, 36–37, 48, 95, *98*, 102, 109–113, 119–120
political roles, 55, 77
on poverty, 110
and protests, 4, 57–60
shooting of, 113–114
speeches of, vii, 7–9, 18, 30–31, 66, 77, 97, 99–100, 108
travels, 83–84
on the Vietnam War, 84–86, 88
and the War on Poverty, 78
Kennedy, Rose, *35*
Kennedy, Ted, 106, 130
Kennedy family, *33–35*, *34*, 74–75
Kennedy King Memorial Initiative, 131
Kerner Commission, 6, 88, 119, 126
King, A. D., 20–21, 52